Numerical
Concentration Test (NCT)

www.How2Become.com

As part of this product you
have also received FREE access to
online tests that will help you to pass
the Numerical Concentration Test.

To gain access, simply go to:

www.PsychometricTestsOnline.co.uk

Get more products for passing
any test or interview at:

www.how2become.com

Orders: Please contact How2become Ltd, Suite 2, 50 Churchill Square Business Centre, Kings Hill, Kent ME19 4YU.

You can order through Amazon.co.uk under ISBN 978-1-910602-17-1, via the website www.How2Become.com or through Gardners.com.

ISBN: 978-1-910602-17-1

First published in 2015 by How2become Ltd.

Typeset for How2become Ltd by Anton Pshinka.

Printed in Great Britain for How2become Ltd by: CMP (uk) Limited, Poole, Dorset.

Disclaimer

Every effort has been made to ensure that the information contained within this guide is accurate at the time of publication. How2become Ltd is not responsible for anyone failing any part of any selection process as a result of the information contained within this guide. How2become Ltd and their authors cannot accept any responsibility for any errors or omissions within this guide, however caused. No responsibility for loss or damage occasioned by any person acting, or refraining from action, as a result of the material in this publication can be accepted by How2become Ltd.

The information within this guide does not represent the views of any third party service or organisation.

CONTENTS

INTRODUCTION

INTRODUCTION TO YOUR NEW GUIDE

Welcome to your new guide, Numerical Concentration Tests. This guide contains 100s of pages of sample questions for you to work through, which will ultimately provide you with the best practice and preparation to pass your assessment.

Here at How2become, we have done our utmost to ensure you have a guide packed full of practice questions in order for you to better your knowledge regarding the Numerical Concentration Tests.

The Numerical Concentration Test is designed to assess a candidate's ability to work swiftly through lots of questions that require a great level of concentration and a strong eye for detail.

The key to success is to try your hardest to get 100% in the test you are undertaking. If you aim for 100% in your preparation, then you are far more likely to achieve the career that you want.

This preparation guide deliberately supplies you with lots of sample questions to assist you through your preparation stages, prior to that all important assessment. A Numerical Concentration Test usually consists of 150 questions, which is to be completed in the time frame of 5 minutes. However, it is highly unlikely that you will be able to complete all 150 questions. You probably won't even be able to complete half of the testing questions; so it is important to understand what to expect in your actual assessment, in order to successfully pass the assessment.

We have provided plenty of practice questions to allow you to focus not only on answering the questions, but the time limit as well. We want to ensure you a worthwhile guide that is guaranteed to better your testing scores!

Good luck and best wishes.

The how2become team

The How2become team

STRUCTURE OF YOUR GUIDE

This book follows a very clear and simple structure in order to make the most out of your Numerical Concentration testing guide.

Our aim is to make sure that you are provided with enough practice and preparation prior to your assessment.

This Numerical Concentration testing guide follows the structure as formulated below:

- Introduction – introducing your new guide
- About the Numerical Concentration Test
  - o Useful tips and advice for your assessment
- Numerical Concentration Test – Practice
  - o 50 practice questions
  - o Visual answers
- Numerical Concentration Test - Section 1.
- Numerical Concentration Test - Section 2
- Numerical Concentration Test - Section 3
- Numerical Concentration Test - Section 4
- Numerical Concentration Test - Section 5
- Numerical Concentration Test - Section 6
- Numerical Concentration Test - Section 7
- Numerical Concentration Test - Section 8
  - o 150 questions to be completed in 5 minutes
  - o Visual answers
- A Few Final Words…

ABOUT
Numerical
Concentration
TESTS

ABOUT NUMERICAL CONCENTRATION TESTS

Numerical Concentration Tests are a form of assessment which are designed to measure a candidate's ability and proficiency at comparing combinations of digits, and determine which combination of digits is not the same.

The test itself can be assessed in two ways. Firstly, some companies use a numerical comparison test which uses sets of numbers, and you have to find the digits that do not match. Whereas other tests focus on alpha-numerical digits which comprise of letters and numbers. Both types of tests assess the same thing in terms of concentration and time keeping skills.

WHAT TO EXPECT

The Numerical Concentration Test is generally an online assessment whereby you will be given four combinations of pairs. This will either be four combinations of number digits, or a mixture of letters and numbers. Your job is to find the pair that does not match in both columns.

An example below is illustrated so you can visualise what to expect:

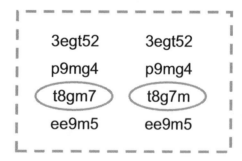

The test is simple. All you have to do is spot which pair does not match. In the above example, the row that does not match is highlighted. You should be able to notice that the reason this combination does not match is because the 'm' and the '7' are in different places in both rows.

For the test, you will be given 5 minutes in which to answer 150 questions. The key to the test is to work swiftly and accurately. The test is designed so that you are unable to finish it, so do not be put off by the thought of not being able to complete your assessment.

HOW CAN I PREPARE?

Your performance in a Numerical Concentration Test can undoubtedly be bettered through practice! Getting to grips with the format of the test, and gaining an insight of the typical questions you are likely to face can only work to your advantage.

The more you practice, the more you will see your performance excel! With any psychometric test, it is important to fully maximise your skills and knowledge prior to your assessment to ensure the best result.

This comprehensive guide will provide you with lots of sample questions, similar to those you can expect to find on your Numerical Concentration Test.

Our insightful and ultimate preparation guide will allow you to grasp the style of the test, understand what is expected, and provide you with all the preparataion tools needed to complete the test.

Please note, that whether you are sitting a Numerical Concentration Test which contains only numbers, or whether it is a test based on alpha-numerical digits, the test requires the same level of concentration, perservance and proficieny. If you practice both types of tests, you are guaranteed to increase your chances of success and thus, better your performance!

TIME LIMITS

You will be given 5 minutes in which to answer 150 questions. Now, this may seem relatively far-fetched to complete 150 questions in only 300 seconds, but the test is designed so you are unable to finish it. Ultimately, you want to aim for speed as well as accuracy.

WHAT DOES THIS TEST MEASURE?

Fundamentally, a Numerical Concentration Test assesses a candidate's ability to compare information, and find the error amongst that information. Moreover, this test also focuses on:

- Attention to detail
- Good concentration
- Proficiency
- Great timing skills

WHO TAKES A NUMERICAL VISUAL COMPARISON TEST?

A Numerical Concentration Test is used in a variety of job application processes. Predominantly, many train operating companies use this assessment as a pre-screening process to determine candidates who are likely to be successful further down the line of their job application.

The test is typically used by Train Operating Companies (TOC's) as part of their recruitment process.

Note, that not only train driving companies use this type of test as part of their recruitment process. Other companies use a variety of psychometric testing, and it is important to fully comprehend the expectations required to successfully complete these types of testing.

PASS MARK

The pass mark for the Numerical Concentration Test is difficult to determine exactly. The majority of candidate's who successfully pass, border the pass mark of 50 correct questions out of the possible 150. This is based on 50 answers that are almost all correct with minimal errors.

Prior to your assessment, you should go into the test with an optimistic approach. Try and aim for 100%. The higher you aim for, the more likely you will score higher marks. Going into your Numerical Concentration Test, or any other test for that means, in a positive mind-set, can only work to your advantage. If you were to go into a test with the mind-set of negative thoughts, you are less likely to achieve high marks.

STRUCTURE OF THE BOOK

The book is laid out in a simple format to ensure you are able to make the most of your testing guide.

Each test will either focus on a numerical comparison, or an alpha-numerical comparison test. These tests are mixed up throughout the book to ensure you gain the best result. Ultimately, the more you practice, the more likely you are to succeed.

GENERAL TIPS
FOR NUMERICAL
CONCENTRATION
TEST

GENERAL TIPS FOR THE NUMERICAL CONCENTRATION TEST

- When taking the actual test, use a computer mouse to select your answers as opposed to a touchpad. You need to be able to move around the screen quickly and effectively. Using a touchpad is harder to control, and therefore will slow you up in the process.

- Make sure you drink plenty of water prior to your assessment. Ensure that you are fully hydrated in order to improve your concentration levels.

- Preparation is crucial! Before sitting your real assessment, make sure you take the time to fully prepare for your test. The more you practice, the more likely you are to achieve better marks.

- Make sure that you practice these questions under timed conditions. Not only do you have to work on getting the answers correct, but the time limit is extremely restrictive, and thus you want to work on your timing skills in order to stand a better chance at passing.

- Practising under strict timed conditions is an important part of the preparation! Remember, the test will require you to answer 150 questions in 5 minutes, and although the majority of people do not finish the test, you need to be able to work swiftly through each question. The only way you can better your timing skills, is simply through practising!

- This may seem relatively obvious, but making sure you get a good night's sleep the night before your real test will work to your advantage. Getting a good night's sleep not only makes you feel better and more awake, but it will allow you to feel fully concentrated and fully aware in order to perform at your best.

- It is crucial that your main priority is accuracy as well as speed. You will notice that the first few sets of questions, you will find that you have good concentration levels, but as the test goes on, you will find it more difficult to distinguish between the combinations of digits, and so you need to work on your concentration skills.

- Whether you are required to sit a Numerical Concentration Test based on numbers or alpha-numbers; both styles of tests assess the same thing. So, in order to become more proficient at these tests, it is best to revise both styles to increase your chances of success.

- Make sure that on the morning of your assessment, you eat a healthy breakfast. Your breakfast should be packed full of vitamins and all the essential nutrients required to perform at your best level. A good balanced breakfast in the morning could be weetabix with bananas, or porridge; both containing essential carbohydrates, iron and calcium.

- Don't guess answers! It is better to have answered 50 questions and got them all right, as opposed to answering 80 questions and getting 30 wrong. The fact that you will feel like you're running out of time is no reason to rush through the questions. This will only sacrfie your accuracy, and thus will impact on your results.

Finally, we have also provided you with some additional free online psychometric tests which will help to further improve your competence in this particular testing area. To gain access, simply go to:

www.PsychometricTestsOnline.co.uk

Good luck and best wishes,

The how2become team

The How2become team

PRACTICE
TEST

(You will be given **50 practice questions** to work through. If you want to work to a time limit, complete these questions in **1 minute and 40 seconds** – this is the approximate time limit you would get to spend on 1/3 of the test).

This is a practice section, so you may want to try these questions without using a time limit.

Look at the four pairs of alpha-numerical digits. Circle or highlight the combination pair that **does not** match.

Sheet 1

e4gh6	e4gh6	flg72	flg72	le93n0	le93no	fk238f	fk238f
mf85f	mf85f	w23tn	we3tn	mfgk3	mfgk3	sh389t	sh389t
er6u8	er68u	mee82	mee82	fgk69	fgk69	flt04j	ftl04j
s45g4	s45g4	cmlo3	cmlo3	df3j9	df3j9	ti06m	ti06m
22946	22946	mgfro	mgfro	ffr48l	ffr48l	ee59g	ee59g
asmto	asmto	fl305g	f305g	mepg0	mepg0	fle39f	fle39f
vbnlo	vbnlo	fgmc9	fgmc9	24hjf	24hjj	we239	we239
40i35	40l35	dfo49	dfo49	935ou	935ou	205njd	205ddd
446hre	446hre	cwwo3	cwwo3	cwwo3	cwwo3	cmcw3	cmcw3
30dl25	30dl25	d0034	d0034	d0034	d0034	fp359	fp359
hk59s	hkl9s	20r3jd	20r3jd	20r3jd	20r3jd	ewe03	eew03
dmp4i	dmp4i	d205j	d205y	d205j	d205y	0lyk5	0lyk5
bmlrt4	bmlrt4	33924	33924	trorms	trorms	awo38	awo38
39fm3	39fm3	33912	39912	wotmd	wotmd	cms03	cmso3
fnj22	fnj22	04816	04816	cmwor	cwmor	elcfp8	elcfp8
d239f	d239	30727	30727	wpjkf	wpjkf	d39d3	d39d3
s2gg5	s2gj5	d3ul8v	d3ul8v	vmpsd	vmpsd	ee02ls	eo02ls
l7vf2	l7vf2	kll93e	kli93e	d3ekp4	d3ekp4	dld39	dld39
xcv36	xcv36	cm30f	cm30f	cmc34	ccm34	cmoef3	cmoef3
as26j	as26j	x40fk3	x40fk3	rrmk4	rrmk4	vmko3	vmko3
39fm34	39fm34	r1018f	r1018f	nnro38	nnro38	je02ld	je02ld
vmdf2	vmdf2	lcp383	lcp383	dkd38d	dkd83d	epe02k	epe00k
drr302	drr023	c27ele	c27ele	lsp28d	lsp28d	cvot49	cvot49
eepr48	eepr48	cepep2	ceeep2	amc84	amc84	gfhl49	gfhl49
yu84f	yu84f	zy6dho	zy6dho	gkr9rj	gkr9rj	57mf30	57fm30
p230cl	p23ocl	h54ttw	h54tww	dkpdw	dkpdw	34kg4y	34kg4y
dr3k0	dr3k0	nt457j	nt457j	354985	354995	459782	459782
jyuk05	jyuk05	g4rw3	g4rw3	247693	247693	vmo38	vmo38

*Look at the four pairs of alpha-numerical digits. Circle or highlight the combination pair that **does not** match.*

Sheet 2

59683	59683	loov9	loov9	he939	he939	q04mv	q04mv
flm49	flm49	eeo39	eeo93	13053	13053	plcm53	plcm35
vm34	vm43	eeor3	eeor3	jflr3r	jlfr3r	rrp03l	rrp031
mpd2f	mpd2f	vmfk3	vmfk3	eeop2	eeop2	bc92l	bc921

03957	09357	mclrp	mclrp	g47un	g47un	xlrpyh	xlrpyh
18475	18475	w02kr	w02kr	qp2305	qp2305	fmvlt3	fmvlt3
38506	38506	empf9	empf9	rpmb8	rpmbb	vm39r	vm39e
90184	90184	vmblf	vmbfl	ghrp23	ghrp23	vrk45	vrk45

35856	35856	79954	79554	kal39	kal39	764053	764053
vl456	vi456	tie92	tie92	dl359	dl359	gk4924	gk4924
e569g	e569g	pql48	pql48	c3n95	c3m95	dk5023	dk5033
f40gl	f40gl	mp02	mp02	f39ut	f39ut	epl495	epl495

loop29	loop29	30598	30598	qprity	qprity	ld903f	ld003f
ei358e	el358e	12368	12368	gdladg	gldadg	qorf83	qorf83
xwo48	xwo48	08642	08642	vnxfd	vnxfd	cm489	cm489
3598fj	3598fj	02578	02758	04684	04684	fk4n8	fk4n8

jdla93	ldla93	3597fs	3597fs	368734	368734	qp295k	qp295k
cm947d	cm947d	lanm9	lanm9	venk52	venk52	ri38fm	ri38fm
dl39fr	dl39fr	z19dk1	zl9dk1	235078	235078	sloe03	slope03
fj2305	fj2305	a024k	a024k	ceknt3	cenmt3	2305fo	2305fo

35897	35897	dmoove	dmoove
13098	13098	plan39	plan39
57302	57032	squir3	squirt
09834	09834	49fkvs	49fkvs

ANSWERS TO *PRACTICE TEST*

Sheet 1

e4gh6	e4gh6	flg72	flg72	le93n0	le93no	fk238f	fk238f
mf85f	mf85f	w23tn	we3tn	mfgk3	mfgk3	sh389t	sh389t
er6u8	er68u	mee82	mee82	fgk69	fgk69	flt04j	ftl04j
s45g4	s45g4	cmlo3	cmlo3	df3j9	df3j9	ti06m	ti06m

22946	22946	mgfro	mgfro	ffr48l	ffr48l	ee59g	ee59g
asmto	asmto	fl305g	f305g	mepg0	mepg0	fle39f	fle39f
vbnlo	vbnlo	fgmc9	fgmc9	24hjf	24hjj	we239	we239
40i35	40l35	dfo49	dfo49	935ou	935ou	205njd	205ddd

446hre	446hre	cwwo3	cwwo3	cwwo3	cwwo3	cmcw3	cmcw3
30dl25	30dl25	d0034	d0034	d0034	d0034	fp359	fp359
hk59s	hkl9s	20r3jd	20r3jd	20r3jd	20r3jd	ewe03	eew03
dmp4i	dmp4i	d205j	d205y	d205j	d205y	0lyk5	0lyk5

bmlrt4	bmlrt4	33924	33924	trorms	trorms	awo38	awo38
39fm3	39fm3	33912	39912	wotmd	wotmd	cms03	cmso3
fnj22	fnj22	04816	04816	cmwor	cwmor	elcfp8	elcfp8
d239f	d239	30727	30727	wpjkf	wpjkf	d39d3	d39d3

s2gg5	s2gj5	d3ul8v	d3ul8v	vmpsd	vmpsd	ee02ls	eo02ls
l7vf2	l7vf2	kll93e	kli93e	d3ekp4	d3ekp4	dld39	dld39
xcv36	xcv36	cm30f	cm30f	cmc34	ccm34	cmoef3	cmoef3
as26j	as26j	x40fk3	x40fk3	rrmk4	rrmk4	vmko3	vmko3

39fm34	39fm34	r1018f	r1018f	nnro38	nnro38	je02ld	je02ld
vmdf2	vmdf2	lcp383	lcp383	dkd38d	dkd83d	epe02k	epe00k
drr302	drr023	c27ele	c27ele	lsp28d	lsp28d	cvot49	cvot49
eepr48	eepr48	cepep2	ceeep2	amc84	amc84	gfhl49	gfhl49

yu84f	yu84f	zy6dho	zy6dho	gkr9rj	gkr9rj	57mf30	57fm30
p230cl	p23ocl	h54ttw	h54tww	dkpdw	dkpdw	34kg4y	34kg4y
dr3k0	dr3k0	nt457j	nt457j	354985	354995	459782	459782
jyuk05	jyuk05	g4rw3	g4rw3	247693	247693	vmo38	vmo38

Sheet 2

59683	59683	loov9	loov9	he939	he939	q04mv	q04mv
flm49	flm49	eeo39	eeo93	13053	13053	plcm53	plcm35
vm34	vm43	eeor3	eeor3	jflr3r	jlfr3r	rrp03l	rrp031
mpd2f	mpd2f	vmfk3	vmfk3	eeop2	eeop2	bc92l	bc921
03957	09357	mclrp	mclrp	g47un	g47un	xlrpyh	xlrpyh
18475	18475	w02kr	w02kr	qp2305	qp2305	fmvlt3	fmvlt3
38506	38506	empf9	empf9	rpmb8	rpmbb	vm39r	vm39e
90184	90184	vmblf	vmbfl	ghrp23	ghrp23	vrk45	vrk45
35856	35856	79954	79554	kal39	kal39	764053	764053
vl456	vi456	tie92	tie92	dl359	dl359	gk4924	gk4924
e569g	e569g	pql48	pql48	c3n95	c3m95	dk5023	dk5033
f40gl	f40gl	mp02	mp02	f39ut	f39ut	epl495	epl495
loop29	loop29	30598	30598	qprity	qprity	ld903f	ld003f
ei358e	el358e	12368	12368	gdladg	gldadg	qorf83	qorf83
xwo48	xwo48	08642	08642	vnxfd	vnxfd	cm489	cm489
3598fj	3598fj	02578	02758	04684	04684	fk4n8	fk4n8
jdla93	ldla93	3597fs	3597fs	368734	368734	qp295k	qp295k
cm947d	cm947d	lanm9	lanm9	venk52	venk52	ri38fm	ri38fm
dl39fr	dl39fr	z19dk1	zl9dk1	235078	235078	sloe03	slope03
fj2305	fj2305	a024k	a024k	ceknt3	cenmt3	2305fo	2305fo
35897	35897	dmoove	dmoove				
13098	13098	plan39	plan39				
57302	57032	squir3	squirt				
09834	09834	49fkvs	49fkvs				

TEST 1

(Numerical Comparison)

(You will be given **150 questions** which should be completed using the time limit of **5 minutes**).

*Look at the four pairs of numerical digits. Circle or highlight the combination pair that **does not** match.*

Sheet 1

9871 9871	7431 7431	4976 4676	7923 7293
1235 1235	1225 1255	4697 4697	3265 3265
7469 7496	3664 3664	6562 6562	2647 2647
6344 6344	3549 3549	3597 3597	4961 4961

7947 7947	4697 4697	5591 5591	5598 5598
4654 4564	7989 7989	6694 6694	6659 6659
4165 4165	6278 6278	1622 1662	4613 4613
1346 1346	4691 6691	4448 4448	3108 3018

7952 7952	8853 8853	7792 7792	4598 4598
0097 0097	8469 8669	7913 7931	6621 6621
0064 0664	1465 1465	7469 7469	5648 5648
1025 1025	4812 4812	7692 7692	8712 7812

4564 4564	5684 5684	6541 5641	3369 3369
0694 0694	5479 5479	2658 2658	3478 3478
1620 1620	2698 2698	7952 7952	3589 3859
4169 4196	1610 1601	2679 2679	1694 1694

4644 4444	6523 6523	7943 7943	9376 9376
6646 6646	0042 0042	3246 3246	9713 9713
1366 1366	0170 0070	0651 0551	0544 0544
3024 3024	0394 0394	3651 3651	4369 4339

5478 5478	7410 7410	5525 5525	7410 7401
9631 9631	4987 4987	5571 5571	6314 6314
3260 3260	7631 7613	5987 9587	9874 9874
0587 0857	6854 6854	5103 5103	1679 1679

4622 4622	4103 4103	4792 4792	4967 4667
2264 2624	3034 3034	5423 5423	4610 4610
1325 1325	0950 0590	6432 6432	6459 6459
4679 4679	1463 1463	0649 0469	6462 6462

*Look at the four pairs of numerical digits. Circle or highlight the combination pair that **does not** match.*

Sheet 2

49846 49846	97842 97842	44975 44975	79895 79995
46216 46216	64494 64494	69871 69871	97461 97461
87641 86741	65979 65979	36105 31605	46959 46959
47879 47879	14645 14465	49792 49792	46997 46997
49526 49526	79852 79852	79852 79852	84641 84641
25984 25948	59441 59414	25694 25694	00651 06051
16479 16479	19859 19859	41977 41977	03103 03103
49751 49751	49742 49742	10268 10286	13204 13204
98510 95810	95615 95615	79654 79654	46584 46584
97106 97106	49562 49562	97414 97414	69716 69716
65892 65892	16984 16894	47945 47945	62544 62554
15497 15497	49756 49756	65487 65478	69712 69712
96587 96587	47925 47925	47925 47925	79261 79261
95410 95410	96102 66102	79560 79650	41004 41004
01360 01360	23547 23547	06414 06414	47978 47778
46105 64105	46940 46940	49787 49787	98851 98851
98712 98712	98514 98514	89474 89447	96478 96478
36204 32604	54477 54477	49974 49974	46775 46775
79461 79461	61149 61149	49887 49887	16584 16584
13645 13645	49470 49770	46120 46120	23668 23688
98521 98521	96584 96584	74698 76498	62302 62302
56987 56987	46414 46414	58962 58962	56841 56841
14479 11479	02366 02666	13644 13644	36984 36984
36972 36972	56320 56320	47851 47851	27893 27895
86984 86984	74632 74632	63258 63258	48579 48579
36942 33942	03665 03655	85936 85996	69520 69520
47497 47497	46910 46910	97848 97848	26547 26547
46979 46979	03689 03689	96347 96347	79585 79558

*Look at the four pairs of numerical digits. Circle or highlight the combination pair that **does not** match.*

Sheet 3

494765	494765	498514	498514	796585	796558	798895	798895
498451	498451	497897	497897	874158	874158	498978	498978
469597	469597	798585	795885	895851	895851	479784	479784
798952	799852	568744	568744	498798	498798	154775	154575

745698	745698	798514	798514	467985	476985	498984	498984
798520	798220	498798	498798	598977	598977	465987	465987
795210	795210	798520	798520	789552	789552	495952	499552
462248	462248	795463	795436	469898	469898	798524	798524

798895	798995	794614	794414	978984	978984	978984	978984
798554	798554	498784	498784	494881	494481	465898	465598
498795	498795	978984	978984	497974	497974	741220	741220
495202	495202	798522	798522	499874	499874	023650	023650

798565	798565	498894	498894	794654	794654	795655	795655
565987	565987	794659	794659	469795	469795	746984	746984
477784	477784	895251	895551	465201	465210	468972	468972
465207	465270	465687	465687	469897	469897	136897	136879

741235	741235	968571	968571	698745	699745	741369	741369
869695	869695	146447	146447	596897	596897	699523	699523
579852	579552	797889	797899	798520	798520	232644	232644
265489	265489	568987	568987	236547	236547	465947	465974

794685	794885	465985	465985	794655	794655	798556	798556
856982	856982	598799	598799	565977	655977	565978	565978
003587	003587	798562	798662	798523	798523	798898	798998
594412	594412	265977	265977	265978	265978	895622	895622

895656	896556	562022	562022	699845	699845	798556	798556
569875	569875	226985	226985	565977	565977	565988	565988
331001	331001	450023	450023	788998	788998	787848	787848
012024	012024	232021	232010	595232	595532	487874	787848

Look at the four pairs of numerical digits. Circle or highlight the combination pair that **does not** match.

Sheet 4

8989	8989	9894	9894	7981	7981	79865	79865
9897	9897	4621	4221	1659	1569	49655	49655
7989	7989	0262	0262	5954	5954	41035	41035
5656	5556	4689	4689	4203	4203	56568	56668

79856	79865	46687	46887	79856	79856	95897	95897
56597	56597	79861	79861	26564	26664	46598	46598
46523	46523	46597	46597	49874	49874	79895	79985
26546	26546	79852	79852	10124	10124	59256	59256

7985	7885	7985	7985	79523	79523	59659	59659
5659	5659	1301	1301	25665	25565	49974	49974
8987	8987	3624	3664	59787	59787	49595	49995
7981	7981	4658	4658	25659	25659	26211	26211

59594	59549	62659	62569	62622	62622	46565	46565
46595	46595	49897	49897	62261	62261	56594	56594
98778	98778	79856	79856	12616	12616	46797	46797
46230	46230	62644	62644	64652	46652	13206	12306

46598	46589	56594	56594	49846	49846	5951	5915
89798	89798	42369	42639	56578	56578	2665	2665
89871	89871	66477	66477	78978	87978	5621	5621
13256	13256	56201	56201	95251	95251	1035	1035

2326	2326	2655	2655	7950	7950	7958	7958
5654	5654	5659	5559	1659	1659	2326	2362
4652	4652	7985	7985	8951	9851	2598	2598
2320	2302	4620	4620	4621	4621	7895	7895

23265	23665	46595	46595	56959	56959	59554	59554
56989	56989	78985	78985	65654	65654	46256	46256
89874	89874	56597	56597	13698	31698	98778	98778
43221	43221	74395	74359	78365	78365	95861	98561

*Look at the four pairs of numerical digits. Circle or highlight the combination pair that **does not** match.*

Sheet 5

79534	79334	75364	75346	56523	56523	79583	79583
62987	62987	56871	56871	35654	35654	26565	26565
45654	45654	25657	25657	49762	47962	59874	95874
46547	46547	47982	47982	23210	23210	46489	46489

79582	79582	46598	46958	59562	59562	46253	46253
26295	26295	89532	89532	26249	26249	23266	23266
98974	98974	23264	23264	98955	98855	59775	57975
36230	36330	46479	46479	56215	56215	45645	45645

46958	64958	46522	46522	56222	56222	25655	25655
89872	89872	23679	23679	26998	26988	59879	59879
32697	32697	98746	98476	89745	89745	79789	79889
46575	46575	56597	56597	16568	16568	59977	59977

79586	79586	2565	2565	4956	4956	4656	4656
56595	56595	5657	5667	2654	2654	5978	5978
97955	97955	7985	7985	4659	4659	0035	0035
56597	65597	2362	2362	7985	4659	0610	0601

65654	65654	4658	4658	49522	49552	84764	84764
20364	20364	8985	8895	26548	26548	46597	46597
03654	03654	2697	2697	89775	89775	98523	98523
13034	13304	7985	7985	26459	26459	23265	32265

46579	46579	45955	45955	59584	59584	79562	79562
89875	89855	56577	56577	59532	55532	26541	25541
26204	26204	98956	98966	23264	23264	49897	49897
89531	89531	26289	26289	46547	46547	79852	79852

79582	79582	97855	97855	79582	79582	79565	79565
26297	26297	56597	56597	26654	26654	56597	56597
79853	79853	79526	79562	49656	49656	74151	71451
26259	22659	26256	26256	26597	26579	26597	26597

*Look at the four pairs of numerical digits. Circle or highlight the combination pair that **does not** match.*

Sheet 6

957422	957422	798552	798552	795862	975862	46956	46956
262594	265294	268975	268975	262949	262949	52695	52695
479562	479562	565102	565102	498952	498952	59722	57922
262449	262449	· 236264	236246	236297	236297	26594	26594

49562	49562	995525	995525	79525	79525	79855	79855
26974	26974	565987	565978	26978	26978	89512	89512
16981	61981	798553	798553	79820	79820	45847	45847
16595	16595	236269	236269	16597	61597	78474	78874

79582	79582	79526	79256
26547	26457	56597	56597
12305	12305	79526	79526
54597	54597	56597	56597

ANSWERS TO *TEST 1*

Sheet 1

9871 9871	7431 7431	4976 4676	7923 7293
1235 1235	1225 1255	4697 4697	3265 3265
7469 7496	3664 3664	6562 6562	2647 2647
6344 6344	3549 3549	3597 3597	4961 4961

7947 7947	4697 4697	5591 5591	5598 5598
4654 4564	7989 7989	6694 6694	6659 6659
4165 4165	6278 6278	1622 1662	4613 4613
1346 1346	4691 6691	4448 4448	3108 3018

7952 7952	8853 8853	7792 7792	4598 4598
0097 0097	8469 8669	7913 7931	6621 6621
0064 0664	1465 1465	7469 7469	5648 5648
1025 1025	4812 4812	7692 7692	8712 7812

4564 4564	5684 5684	6541 5641	3369 3369
0694 0694	5479 5479	2658 2658	3478 3478
1620 1620	2698 2698	7952 7952	3589 3859
4169 4196	1610 1601	2679 2679	1694 1694

4644 4444	6523 6523	7943 7943	9376 9376
6646 6646	0042 0042	3246 3246	9713 9713
1366 1366	0170 0070	0651 0551	0544 0544
3024 3024	0394 0394	3651 3651	4369 4339

5478 5478	7410 7410	5525 5525	7410 7401
9631 9631	4987 4987	5571 5571	6314 6314
3260 3260	7631 7613	5987 9587	9874 9874
0587 0857	6854 6854	5103 5103	1679 1679

4622 4622	4103 4103	4792 4792	4967 4667
2264 2624	3034 3034	5423 5423	4610 4610
1325 1325	0950 0590	6432 6432	6459 6459
4679 4679	1463 1463	0649 0469	6462 6462

Sheet 2

49846	49846	97842	97842	44975	44975	79895	79995
46216	46216	64494	64494	69871	69871	97461	97461
87641	86741	65979	65979	36105	31605	46959	46959
47879	47879	14645	14465	49792	49792	46997	46997

49526	49526	79852	79852	79852	79852	84641	84641
25984	25948	59441	59414	25694	25694	00651	06051
16479	16479	19859	19859	41977	41977	03103	03103
49751	49751	49742	49742	10268	10286	13204	13204

98510	95810	95615	95615	79654	79654	46584	46584
97106	97106	49562	49562	97414	97414	69716	69716
65892	65892	16984	16894	47945	47945	62544	62554
15497	15497	49756	49756	65487	65478	69712	69712

96587	96587	47925	47925	47925	47925	79261	79261
95410	95410	96102	66102	79560	79650	41004	41004
01360	01360	23547	23547	06414	06414	47978	47778
46105	64105	46940	46940	49787	49787	98851	98851

98712	98712	98514	98514	89474	89447	96478	96478
36204	32604	54477	54477	49974	49974	46775	46775
79461	79461	61149	61149	49887	49887	16584	16584
13645	13645	49470	49770	46120	46120	23668	23688

98521	98521	96584	96584	74698	76498	62302	62302
56987	56987	46414	46414	58962	58962	56841	56841
14479	11479	02366	02666	13644	13644	36984	36984
36972	36972	56320	56320	47851	47851	27893	27895

86984	86984	74632	74632	63258	63258	48579	48579
36942	33942	03665	03655	85936	85996	69520	69520
47497	47497	46910	46910	97848	97848	26547	26547
46979	46979	03689	03689	96347	96347	79585	79558

Sheet 3

494765	494765	498514	498514	796585	796558	798895	798895
498451	498451	497897	497897	874158	874158	498978	498978
469597	469597	798585	795885	895851	895851	479784	479784
798952	799852	568744	568744	498798	498798	154775	154575
745698	745698	798514	798514	467985	476985	498984	498984
798520	798220	498798	498798	598977	598977	465987	465987
795210	795210	798520	798520	789552	789552	495952	499552
462248	462248	795463	795436	469898	469898	798524	798524
798895	798995	794614	794414	978984	978984	978984	978984
798554	798554	498784	498784	494881	494481	465898	465598
498795	498795	978984	978984	497974	497974	741220	741220
495202	495202	798522	798522	499874	499874	023650	023650
798565	798565	498894	498894	794654	794654	795655	795655
565987	565987	794659	794659	469795	469795	746984	746984
477784	477784	895251	895551	465201	465210	468972	468972
465207	465270	465687	465687	469897	469897	136897	136879
741235	741235	968571	968571	698745	699745	741369	741369
869695	869695	146447	146447	596897	596897	699523	699523
579852	579552	797889	797899	798520	798520	232644	232644
265489	265489	568987	568987	236547	236547	465947	465974
794685	794885	465985	465985	794655	794655	798556	798556
856982	856982	598799	598799	565977	655977	565978	565978
003587	003587	798562	798662	798523	798523	798898	798998
594412	594412	265977	265977	265978	265978	895622	895622
895656	896556	562022	562022	699845	699845	798556	798556
569875	569875	226985	226985	565977	565977	565988	565988
331001	331001	450023	450023	788998	788998	787848	787848
012024	012024	232021	232010	595232	595532	487874	787848

Sheet 4

8989	8989	9894	9894	7981	7981	79865	79865
9897	9897	4621	4221	1659	1569	49655	49655
7989	7989	0262	0262	5954	5954	41035	41035
5656	5556	4689	4689	4203	4203	56568	56668

79856	79865	46687	46887	79856	79856	95897	95897
56597	56597	79861	79861	26564	26664	46598	46598
46523	46523	46597	46597	49874	49874	79895	79985
26546	26546	79852	79852	10124	10124	59256	59256

7985	7885	7985	7985	79523	79523	59659	59659
5659	5659	1301	1301	25665	25565	49974	49974
8987	8987	3624	3664	59787	59787	49595	49995
7981	7981	4658	4658	25659	25659	26211	26211

59594	59549	62659	62569	62622	62622	46565	46565
46595	46595	49897	49897	62261	62261	56594	56594
98778	98778	79856	79856	12616	12616	46797	46797
46230	46230	62644	62644	64652	46652	13206	12306

46598	46589	56594	56594	49846	49846	5951	5915
89798	89798	42369	42639	56578	56578	2665	2665
89871	89871	66477	66477	78978	87978	5621	5621
13256	13256	56201	56201	95251	95251	1035	1035

2326	2326	2655	2655	7950	7950	7958	7958
5654	5654	5659	5559	1659	1659	2326	2362
4652	4652	7985	7985	8951	9851	2598	2598
2320	2302	4620	4620	4621	4621	7895	7895

23265	23665	46595	46595	56959	56959	59554	59554
56989	56989	78985	78985	65654	65654	46256	46256
89874	89874	56597	56597	13698	31698	98778	98778
43221	43221	74395	74359	78365	78365	95861	98561

Sheet 5

79534　79334	75364　75346	56523　56523	79583　79583
62987　62987	56871　56871	35654　35654	26565　26565
45654　45654	25657　25657	49762　47962	59874　95874
46547　46547	47982　47982	23210　23210	46489　46489

79582　79582	46598　46958	59562　59562	46253　46253
26295　26295	89532　89532	26249　26249	23266　23266
98974　98974	23264　23264	98955　98855	59775　57975
36230　36330	46479　46479	56215　56215	45645　45645

46958　64958	46522　46522	56222　56222	25655　25655
89872　89872	23679　23679	26998　26988	59879　59879
32697　32697	98746　98476	89745　89745	79789　79889
46575　46575	56597　56597	16568　16568	59977　59977

79586　79586	2565　2565	4956　4956	4656　4656
56595　56595	5657　5667	2654　2654	5978　5978
97955　97955	7985　7985	4659　4659	0035　0035
56597　65597	2362　2362	7985　4659	0610　0601

65654　65654	4658　4658	49522　49552	84764　84764
20364　20364	8985　8895	26548　26548	46597　46597
03654　03654	2697　2697	89775　89775	98523　98523
13034　13304	7985　7985	26459　26459	23265　32265

46579　46579	45955　45955	59584　59584	79562　79562
89875　89855	56577　56577	59532　55532	26541　25541
26204　26204	98956　98966	23264　23264	49897　49897
89531　89531	26289　26289	46547　46547	79852　79852

79582　79582	97855　97855	79582　79582	79565　79565
26297　26297	56597　56597	26654　26654	56597　56597
79853　79853	79526　79562	49656　49656	74151　71451
26259　22659	26256　26256	26597　26579	26597　26597

Sheet 6

957422	957422	798552	798552	795862	975862	46956	46956
262594	265294	268975	268975	262949	262949	52695	52695
479562	479562	565102	565102	498952	498952	59722	57922
262449	262449	236264	236246	236297	236297	26594	26594

49562	49562	995525	995525	79525	79525	79855	79855
26974	26974	565987	565978	26978	26978	89512	89512
16981	61981	798553	798553	79820	79820	45847	45847
16595	16595	236269	236269	16597	61597	78474	78874

79582	79582	79526	79256
26547	26457	56597	56597
12305	12305	79526	79526
54597	54597	56597	56597

TEST 2

(Numerical Comparison)

(You will be given **150 questions** which should be completed using the time limit of **5 minutes**).

Look at the four pairs of numerical digits. Circle or highlight the combination pair that **does not** match.

Sheet 1

7956	9756	7952	7952	7944	7944	7950	7950
4654	4654	6997	6997	2629	2669	2697	2697
6594	6594	9892	9882	8502	8502	7982	7982
9872	9872	2600	2600	5987	5987	2698	2689
7952	7952	7952	7952	9562	9526	4953	4953
2657	2657	2326	2326	2654	2654	2659	2659
8798	8798	4694	4649	4622	4622	8987	8887
2620	2260	4698	4698	2367	2367	7952	7952
5952	5952	5947	5947	9795	9795	6529	6592
2626	2266	4955	4955	2658	6258	7985	7985
4987	4987	5698	5698	0544	0544	1658	1658
7952	7952	8954	8945	9897	9897	1469	1469
4956	4956	8987	8987	7951	7951	9456	4956
4597	4597	5256	5526	1698	1698	5977	5977
7952	7925	4620	4620	8971	8971	7995	7995
2669	2669	2698	2698	1127	1172	2659	2659
4956	4956	4697	4697	1036	1036	0641	6041
2697	2697	9795	9985	5897	5897	1617	1617
7951	7951	2698	2698	0464	0446	7952	7952
0367	0376	7951	7951	2657	2657	0659	0659
4972	4972	7102	7102	7946	9746	7952	7952
2679	2679	2687	2687	1649	1649	2647	2647
5978	5987	4952	4922	7951	7951	7953	7593
9891	9891	0625	0625	2648	2648	0264	0264
5954	5954	4725	4725	7915	7951	4912	4912
2697	2679	0659	0659	3698	3698	2987	2987
3679	3679	8974	9874	7984	7984	7985	7985
3255	3255	1659	1659	1657	1657	2659	2695

Look at the four pairs of numerical digits. Circle or highlight the combination pair that **does not** match.

Sheet 2

26221	26221	49589	49879	49897	49897	49587	49587
45987	54987	49788	49788	58952	58952	79526	79526
79526	79526	59598	59598	29598	92598	26297	26927
26987	26987	89532	89532	79852	79852	79581	79581

69578	69578	79595	79595	49846	49846	78952	88952
89526	89526	89874	89874	65987	65987	06297	06297
65697	65697	46922	46922	49287	49278	79852	79852
98955	89955	59877	59787	95120	95120	06579	06579

49526	49526	79526	79526	49562	49562	79562	79562
67942	67942	26779	26779	26597	26579	26589	26589
36957	36957	65105	65150	79582	79582	79526	79526
79520	79502	49785	49785	25957	25957	26997	26979

79529	79592	59563	59563	79885	79885	49795	49795
59872	59872	78966	78966	26972	26972	26984	26984
26979	26979	78925	78965	26997	62997	49520	49520
95878	95878	39875	39875	62065	62065	29578	29587

45952	45952	74628	74628	49795	49795	49587	94587
98794	98794	59532	55932	26304	26304	59852	59852
36489	36489	26487	26487	79852	79852	23264	23264
66448	64648	79561	79561	26297	26279	49875	49875

98952	98952	49526	49526	79582	79582	49878	49878
26984	26994	26597	26597	26978	26978	69795	69795
49562	49562	79810	78910	79556	79566	59871	59871
19894	19894	06094	06094	56594	56594	06578	60578

59526	55926	45978	45978	79321	79321	14995	14995
62548	62548	26544	26454	23940	23904	89814	89814
02645	02645	79453	79453	26048	26048	19632	19632
10594	10594	13258	13258	06585	06585	26959	26599

Look at the four pairs of numerical digits. Circle or highlight the combination pair that **does not** match.

Sheet 3

59547	59547	49898	49898	59547	59547	49562	49652
59594	59994	59521	59521	36985	36985	23626	23626
49987	49987	49636	94636	26245	22245	49879	49879
79820	79820	49875	49875	50267	50267	46210	46210

6259	6259	4985	4985	4957	4957	47952	47952
5959	5959	2954	2945	9562	9562	26294	26924
7985	9785	4987	4987	2627	2672	79582	79582
2625	2625	1020	1020	7981	7981	26297	26297

49594	94594	49595	49595	45695	45695	56595	56595
49872	49872	29877	29877	59887	59887	55977	55797
26987	26987	78945	78945	79562	79562	78451	78451
79562	79562	18787	18887	26987	29687	18598	18598

4620	4620	7952	7952	79522	79252	45695	45695
2695	6295	2695	2695	26878	26878	59741	59741
3975	3975	7762	7726	78762	78762	05144	05144
3971	3971	0136	0136	26649	26649	48740	47840

45695	45695	79856	79856	46547	46547	94695	94695
45788	45878	26971	26971	26298	26289	26541	26541
98522	98522	16026	16206	89523	89523	01259	10259
02154	02154	56987	56987	32647	32647	79525	79525

47987	47789	49562	49562	47952	47952	79526	79526
46259	46259	26967	62967	26958	26958	56978	56798
89856	89856	79565	79565	89871	89871	79812	79812
26587	26587	56597	56597	16598	61598	16164	16164

4953	4953	4957	4957	7954	7994	46956	46956
6106	6106	7956	7965	1959	1959	26526	26526
5998	5989	6298	6298	9515	9515	46956	46596
4695	4695	7951	7951	6956	6956	16625	16625

*Look at the four pairs of numerical digits. Circle or highlight the combination pair that **does not** match.*

Sheet 4

495962 495962	792506 792506	134657 134657	165498 165498
265548 265548	648621 648621	579156 579516	898632 898632
499856 498956	985614 895614	461227 461227	265479 264579
565654 565654	465975 465975	756798 756798	795612 795612

987659 987569	469579 469579	495631 495631	469562 469562
974064 974064	943146 493146	146476 146476	656545 656545
364896 364896	346439 346439	659782 659782	963272 936272
647820 647820	124057 124057	332016 332061	120368 120368

465653 465563	695653 695653	495652 495652	495762 495762
327985 327985	369745 369745	232264 322264	968421 968421
361410 361410	456958 456958	469789 469789	023058 020358
979862 979862	565410 565401	203246 203246	875653 875653

496562 496562	989523 989532	465620 465620	479562 749562
658978 658987	659874 659874	236988 326988	356445 356445
746982 746982	456025 456025	898741 898741	289851 289851
456984 456984	620462 620462	136265 136265	629878 629878

462300 462300	795843 795843	794623 794623	795623 795623
656875 656875	367462 364762	465795 465795	462321 462321
794613 794613	128954 128954	986561 986561	120657 126057
135896 315896	367589 367589	213015 123015	036980 036980

479562 475962	469253 469253	795623 795623	795320 795320
845841 845841	232644 232644	469741 469741	256958 256958
463286 463286	031659 301659	283917 283197	476232 476223
236367 236367	123568 123568	461973 461973	794628 794628

956231 956213	496532 496532	469230 469230	479623 479623
632326 632326	236597 236597	326597 326597	265644 265644
795620 795620	444598 444598	795621 759621	623055 623505
065958 065958	632554 632254	165844 165844	112025 112025

*Look at the four pairs of numerical digits. Circle or highlight the combination pair that **does not** match.*

Sheet 5

45478	45478	48952	48925	16645	16645	49526	49526
79865	79865	29548	29548	26594	26954	45695	45695
62610	62610	48145	48145	49897	49897	26548	26458
48879	84879	48778	48778	84514	84514	59540	59540
59564	59564	79562	79562	49589	49589	49579	49579
49878	49878	26589	26598	78992	87992	95214	95214
79556	79555	79514	79514	29018	29018	46498	46498
56201	56201	14698	14698	48405	48405	95212	95221
14957	14957	49597	49597	49784	49784	79526	79526
89566	89565	59059	59059	29852	29852	29578	29578
56424	56424	01462	01462	26014	26041	47841	47841
98970	98970	02649	20649	49878	49878	15887	15587
49562	94562	44926	44926	49875	49875	90895	90895
26579	26579	65897	65987	69874	69874	59005	59005
89825	89825	79852	79852	16984	61984	98994	98994
26215	26215	26597	26597	49802	49802	94875	94847
79569	79569	79556	75956	46562	46562	49562	49562
59878	59878	56978	56978	65987	65897	00326	00326
57841	57814	79562	79562	79523	79523	46645	64645
16959	16959	26597	26597	26547	26547	79561	79561
47956	47596	49622	49622	46224	46224	49562	49562
26598	26598	29974	29974	49856	49865	26987	26897
79841	79841	49856	49856	59878	59878	79564	79564
13021	13021	29578	92578	62348	62348	46232	46232
14626	14626	74796	77496	46952	46952	49797	49797
59875	95875	26994	26994	79855	79585	46956	46956
49516	49516	79565	79565	79562	79562	26982	26982
62597	62597	56597	56597	26979	26979	26214	26124

Look at the four pairs of numerical digits. Circle or highlight the combination pair that **does not** match.

Sheet 6

79562	97562	47956	47596	49656	49656	49768	49768
25958	25958	26589	26589	26989	26989	86598	86598
79856	79856	79856	79856	79562	79562	89564	98564
56244	56244	59578	59578	62987	26987	46298	46298

79556	79556	41962	41962	79564	97564	16266	16266
59597	59579	29877	29787	46629	46629	46525	46525
79656	79656	79562	79562	97956	97956	89561	89561
59897	59897	26598	26598	56249	56249	46458	46548

49526	49526	49876	49786
59879	59879	56597	56597
78949	78949	79561	79561
97896	97869	16197	16197

ANSWERS TO *TEST 2*

Sheet 1

7956	9756	7952	7952	7944	7944	7950	7950
4654	4654	6997	6997	2629	2669	2697	2697
6594	6594	9892	9882	8502	8502	7982	7982
9872	9872	2600	2600	5987	5987	2698	2689
7952	7952	7952	7952	9562	9526	4953	4953
2657	2657	2326	2326	2654	2654	2659	2659
8798	8798	4694	4649	4622	4622	8987	8887
2620	2260	4698	4698	2367	2367	7952	7952
5952	5952	5947	5947	9795	9795	6529	6592
2626	2266	4955	4955	2658	6258	7985	7985
4987	4987	5698	5698	0544	0544	1658	1658
7952	7952	8954	8945	9897	9897	1469	1469
4956	4956	8987	8987	7951	7951	9456	4956
4597	4597	5256	5526	1698	1698	5977	5977
7952	7925	4620	4620	8971	8971	7995	7995
2669	2669	2698	2698	1127	1172	2659	2659
4956	4956	4697	4697	1036	1036	0641	6041
2697	2697	9795	9985	5897	5897	1617	1617
7951	7951	2698	2698	0464	0446	7952	7952
0367	0376	7951	7951	2657	2657	0659	0659
4972	4972	7102	7102	7946	9746	7952	7952
2679	2679	2687	2687	1649	1649	2647	2647
5978	5987	4952	4922	7951	7951	7953	7593
9891	9891	0625	0625	2648	2648	0264	0264
5954	5954	4725	4725	7915	7951	4912	4912
2697	2679	0659	0659	3698	3698	2987	2987
3679	3679	8974	9874	7984	7984	7985	7985
3255	3255	1659	1659	1657	1657	2659	2695

Sheet 2

26221 26221	49589 49879	49897 49897	49587 49587
45987 54987	49788 49788	58952 58952	79526 79526
79526 79526	59598 59598	29598 92598	26297 26927
26987 26987	89532 89532	79852 79852	79581 79581
69578 69578	79595 79595	49846 49846	78952 88952
89526 89526	89874 89874	65987 65987	06297 06297
65697 65697	46922 46922	49287 49278	79852 79852
98955 89955	59877 59787	95120 95120	06579 06579
49526 49526	79526 79526	49562 49562	79562 79562
67942 67942	26779 26779	26597 26579	26589 26589
36957 36957	65105 65150	79582 79582	79526 79526
79520 79502	49785 49785	25957 25957	26997 26979
79529 79592	59563 59563	79885 79885	49795 49795
59872 59872	78966 78966	26972 26972	26984 26984
26979 26979	78925 78965	26997 62997	49520 49520
95878 95878	39875 39875	62065 62065	29578 29587
45952 45952	74628 74628	49795 49795	49587 94587
98794 98794	59532 55932	26304 26304	59852 59852
36489 36489	26487 26487	79852 79852	23264 23264
66448 64648	79561 79561	26297 26279	49875 49875
98952 98952	49526 49526	79582 79582	49878 49878
26984 26994	26597 26597	26978 26978	69795 69795
49562 49562	79810 78910	79556 79566	59871 59871
19894 19894	06094 06094	56594 56594	06578 60578
59526 55926	45978 45978	79321 79321	14995 14995
62548 62548	26544 26454	23940 23904	89814 89814
02645 02645	79453 79453	26048 26048	19632 19632
10594 10594	13258 13258	06585 06585	26959 26599

Sheet 3

59547	59547	49898	49898	59547	59547	49562	49652
59594	59994	59521	59521	36985	36985	23626	23626
49987	49987	49636	94636	26245	22245	49879	49879
79820	79820	49875	49875	50267	50267	46210	46210

6259	6259	4985	4985	4957	4957	47952	47952
5959	5959	2954	2945	9562	9562	26294	26924
7985	9785	4987	4987	2627	2672	79582	79582
2625	2625	1020	1020	7981	7981	26297	26297

49594	94594	49595	49595	45695	45695	56595	56595
49872	49872	29877	29877	59887	59887	55977	55797
26987	26987	78945	78945	79562	79562	78451	78451
79562	79562	18787	18887	26987	29687	18598	18598

4620	4620	7952	7952	79522	79252	45695	45695
2695	6295	2695	2695	26878	26878	59741	59741
3975	3975	7762	7726	78762	78762	05144	05144
3971	3971	0136	0136	26649	26649	48740	47840

45695	45695	79856	79856	46547	46547	94695	94695
45788	45878	26971	26971	26298	26289	26541	26541
98522	98522	16026	16206	89523	89523	01259	10259
02154	02154	56987	56987	32647	32647	79525	79525

47987	47789	49562	49562	47952	47952	79526	79526
46259	46259	26967	62967	26958	26958	56978	56798
89856	89856	79565	79565	89871	89871	79812	79812
26587	26587	56597	56597	16598	61598	16164	16164

4953	4953	4957	4957	7954	7994	46956	46956
6106	6106	7956	7965	1959	1959	26526	26526
5998	5989	6298	6298	9515	9515	46956	46596
4695	4695	7951	7951	6956	6956	16625	16625

Sheet 4

495962 495962	792506 792506	134657 134657	165498 165498
265548 265548	648621 648621	579156 579516	898632 898632
499856 498956	985614 895614	461227 461227	265479 264579
565654 565654	465975 465975	756798 756798	795612 795612

987659 987569	469579 469579	495631 495631	469562 469562
974064 974064	943146 493146	146476 146476	656545 656545
364896 364896	346439 346439	659782 659782	963272 936272
647820 647820	124057 124057	332016 332061	120368 120368

465653 465563	695653 695653	495652 495652	495762 495762
327985 327985	369745 369745	232264 322264	968421 968421
361410 361410	456958 456958	469789 469789	023058 020358
979862 979862	565410 565401	203246 203246	875653 875653

496562 496562	989523 989532	465620 465620	479562 749562
658978 658987	659874 659874	236988 326988	356445 356445
746982 746982	456025 456025	898741 898741	289851 289851
456984 456984	620462 620462	136265 136265	629878 629878

462300 462300	795843 795843	794623 794623	795623 795623
656875 656875	367462 364762	465795 465795	462321 462321
794613 794613	128954 128954	986561 986561	120657 126057
135896 315896	367589 367589	213015 123015	036980 036980

479562 475962	469253 469253	795623 795623	795320 795320
845841 845841	232644 232644	469741 469741	256958 256958
463286 463286	031659 301659	283917 283197	476232 476223
236367 236367	123568 123568	461973 461973	794628 794628

956231 956213	496532 496532	469230 469230	479623 479623
632326 632326	236597 236597	326597 326597	265644 265644
795620 795620	444598 444598	795621 759621	623055 623505
065958 065958	632554 632254	165844 165844	112025 112025

Sheet 5

45478	45478	48952	48925	16645	16645	49526	49526
79865	79865	29548	29548	26594	26954	45695	45695
62610	62610	48145	48145	49897	49897	26548	26458
48879	84879	48778	48778	84514	84514	59540	59540

59564	59564	79562	79562	49589	49589	49579	49579
49878	49878	26589	26598	78992	87992	95214	95214
79556	79555	79514	79514	29018	29018	46498	46498
56201	56201	14698	14698	48405	48405	95212	95221

14957	14957	49597	49597	49784	49784	79526	79526
89566	89565	59059	59059	29852	29852	29578	29578
56424	56424	01462	01462	26014	26041	47841	47841
98970	98970	02649	20649	49878	49878	15887	15587

49562	94562	44926	44926	49875	49875	90895	90895
26579	26579	65897	65987	69874	69874	59005	59005
89825	89825	79852	79852	16984	61984	98994	98994
26215	26215	26597	26597	49802	49802	94875	94847

79569	79569	79556	75956	46562	46562	49562	49562
59878	59878	56978	56978	65987	65897	00326	00326
57841	57814	79562	79562	79523	79523	46645	64645
16959	16959	26597	26597	26547	26547	79561	79561

47956	47596	49622	49622	46224	46224	49562	49562
26598	26598	29974	29974	49856	49865	26987	26897
79841	79841	49856	49856	59878	59878	79564	79564
13021	13021	29578	92578	62348	62348	46232	46232

14626	14626	74796	77496	46952	46952	49797	49797
59875	95875	26994	26994	79855	79585	46956	46956
49516	49516	79565	79565	79562	79562	26982	26982
62597	62597	56597	56597	26979	26979	26214	26124

Sheet 6

79562	97562	47956	47596	49656	49656	49768	49768
25958	25958	26589	26589	26989	26989	86598	86598
79856	79856	79856	79856	79562	79562	89564	98564
56244	56244	59578	59578	62987	26987	46298	46298

79556	79556	41962	41962	79564	97564	16266	16266
59597	59579	29877	29787	46629	46629	46525	46525
79656	79656	79562	79562	97956	97956	89561	89561
59897	59897	26598	26598	56249	56249	46458	46548

49526	49526	49876	49786
59879	59879	56597	56597
78949	78949	79561	79561
97896	97869	16197	16197

TEST 3

(Alpha-Numerical Comparison)

(You will be given **150 questions** which should be completed using the time limit of **5 minutes**).

*Look at the four pairs of alpha-numerical digits. Circle or highlight the combination pair that **does not** match.*

Sheet 1

dl49f dl49f	39dj5 39dj5	ep395 ep395	elp59 elp59
30f3r 30f3r	qp294 qp294	eptiy petiy	jkow8 jkow8
lo3vr lo3yr	doi39 doi39	39ri3 39ri3	do03r do03r
or35k or35k	d034i d034l	k5o58 k5o58	mlg94 mlg49
move3 move3	39fjw 39fjw	35957 35957	wp20e wp20e
yijn5 yijn5	pyk5k ypk5k	vmpw3 vmpw3	fmog4 fmog4
fkp30 fk3p0	fmv93 fmv93	deok5 deok5	vmpeg mvpeg
deklp deklp	dmp24 dmp24	rpk60 rpk06	204dk 204dk
ri40e ri40e	fjo39 fjo93	wpa10 wpa01	fejmo fejmo
or30r or30r	powe2 powe2	dld93 dld93	308jo 308jo
fk04j fk04j	dk035 dk035	dkv92 dkv92	r30ie r30ie
t40gj t04gj	358fj 358fj	s024k s024k	20oew 20eow
395kr 395kr	fem34 fem34	09668 09668	trjo3 trjo3
mcl39 mci39	dkp30 dkp30	jig7t jij7t	lpeea lpeaa
jlgt0 jlgt0	20dmv 2odmv	o9ubj o9ubj	f3k63 f3k63
r04ir r04ir	dkf30 dkf30	k0i76 k0i76	fpk46 fpk46
tk303 tk303	gfo3k5 gfo3k5	35fe3 35fe3	lr39fp lr39fp
rlpf2 rlfp2	59eu3 59ue3	350dk 350kd	flp30 flp03
flp3d flp3d	34oiro 34oiro	q130e q130e	fro46 fro46
dkp20 dkp20	3058d 3058d	vmlt3 vmlt3	t4240 t4240
gml45 gml45	dwo14 dwo14	35erp 53erp	3fjo3p 3fjo3p
340rk 340rk	304or 304ro	wp24r wp24r	eoo42 eoo42
e2l04 e2i04	092lp 092lp	fm40e fm40e	mv3o4 mv34o
r3k05 r3k05	2dwp2 2dwp2	emp53 emp53	kop94 kop94
f46ju f46ju	roi3q roi3p	aklq9u1 aklq9u1	35fap1 35fpa1
ssu9s ssu9s	249dj 249dj	dkpc96 dkpc96	dl304r dl304r
skp97 skp97	djo07 djo07	bkpw08 bkpw08	cmp29 cmp29
mo906 mo960	hoit7 hoit7	n08dpp no8dpp	rkp30 rkp30

Look at the four pairs of alpha-numerical digits. Circle or highlight the combination pair that **does not** match.

Sheet 2

fdsp2	fdsp2	eok35	eko35	adp53	adp53	aoj53	aoj53
sa245	sa245	dkwp3	dkwp3	sdlp4	sdlp4	vmpt4	vmpt4
dfvm4	dfvm4	wek46	wek46	fnk3k	fnk3k	repk3	repk3
w563g	w536g	kp57d	kp57d	aslk5	asl5k	dwl53	dwi53

5r9t4	5r9t4	359fj	359fj	qk4kg	gk4kg	grkl3	grkl3
grkp4	grkp4	aru95	aru95	fmlfe4	fmlfe4	frk3r	frkr3
gfm35	gfn35	ryy85	ryy85	tkp40	tkp40	vmlf9	vmlf9
dl35jt	dl35jt	a9u47	a9u74	40irjw	40irjw	dpl69	dpl69

fek42	fek42	gh39a	gh39a	the93	the93	g349fn	g349fn
wij3n	wij3n	amm6f	amm6f	tpe38r	tpe38r	fel48r	fel48r
tmp46	tmp46	flk64	fik64	mfep4	mfep4	twnl3	townl3
m35ja	m35ga	polk5	polk5	r39fe	r93fe	rjow3	rjow3

grtlm4	grtlm4	g9345	g9345	euiorw	eiuorw	35992	35992
bvm3r	bvm3r	38702	38702	wero35	wero35	fnsk3	fns23
5jre30	5lre30	etnkd	entkd	gf35ir	gf35ir	39nr3	39nr3
35793	35793	34098	34098	nro3nr	nro3nr	em6l7	em6l7

gfn4nt	gfn4nt	68753	68753	xdkl4	xdkj4	kjhfy	kjhfy
rm3l2	rm321	freojr	freoir	zprli	zprli	hui96	hui96
yml34	yml34	vcmne	vcmne	itu38	itu38	oj97g	0j97g
plghi3	plghi3	35089	35089	nml30	nml30	nlk9t	nlk9t

kgy7f	kgy7f	gdkn4	gdkn4	campt3	campt3	fajioj	fajioj
987jl	987jli	fejio5	fejio5	dfsfm6	dfsfm6	wplai	wplai
mb905	mb905	plhih8	plhih8	gjasp5	gjsap5	caaop	caaop
cyt86r	cyt86r	nkr39	nrk39	hsk64	hsk64	oarji	oarjil

35983	35983	yaok5	yaok5	29082	29028	fla35a	fla35a
20957	60957	iimpy7	iimpy7	qpalfm	qpalfm	al38gh	al38gh
247d9	247d9	gkdpm	gkdmp	mcao4	mcao4	daml46	dami46
ae3k4	ae3k4	3598j	3598j	nb39f	nb39f	faml57	faml57

*Look at the four pairs of alpha-numerical digits. Circle or highlight the combination pair that **does not** match.*

Sheet 3

03ke3	03ke3	d63ju	d63ju	sal35k	sal53k	30irwk	30irwk
xmcl9	xmci9	qpel29	qpel29	oiu48a	oiu48a	ewpe2	wepe2
e3lmr	e3lmr	drlp35	drlp35	m38ak	m38ak	wwekp	wwekp
46lgm	46lgm	nfl3pq	nfl3qp	as29sk	as29sk	2394e	2394e
3580ak	358oak	salp3	salp3	salpt	salpt	cxa4l3	cxa4l3
dasl53	dasl53	rel86	rel86	gdko4	gdko4	l23lr5	l32lr5
adkl34	adkl34	ro35j	ro35g	39dj3	39dj3	tlep4k	tlep4k
gdlok5	gdlok5	lpsa2	lpsa2	vek2k	vekk2	rk4kar	rk4kar
3lp5g	3lp5g	w29di	w29dd	sal238	sal238	etplgf	etpglf
ktgr4	ktgr4	dsko3	dsko3	249716	294716	grmo4	grmo4
5l3j2	5l3i2	hspl2	hspl2	aso2kr	aso2kr	trmeo	trmeo
a90fg	a90fg	k120d	k120d	rek3ko	rek3ko	3048d	3048d
uialpa	uialpa	cemuv	cemuv	yafm4l	yafm4l	49738	94738
apslfm	paslfm	eokwa	eokwa	49frj3	49frj3	42980	42980
dskape	dskape	s2le0e	s2leeo	0ds2j	ods2j	asjoe	asjoe
oial30	oial30	lp30a	lp30a	198dw	198dw	dsok2	dsok2
bnr3if	bnr3if	rei301	rei031	a9dt4	a9dt4	93jd1	93jd1
x20ala	x20ala	aspl11	aspl11	4m6l7	4m6i7	10sk2	10ks2
z19al6	z19al6	pyt94a	pyt94a	ly4pd	ly4pd	ek20p	ek20p
q204ld	g204ld	idsjwa	idsjwa	d3u9r	d3u9r	y02jr	y02jr
s92md	s92md	694fk	694fk	ou92m	ou92m	29ap2k	29ap2k
d19am	d19am	e2i01	e2i01	mc92a	mc92a	dsk2a9	ds2ka9
wpqa0	wpqao	cm30a	mc30a	nap29	nap92	ma02la	ma02la
prm28	prm28	kao2a	kao2a	ka17s	ka17s	a9dk39	a9dk39
k29ak	k29ak	45da7	45da7	op08a	op08a	28ak9	28ak9
7al20	7ai20	92mf2	92mf2	a7rn5	a7rn5	19sk1	19ks1
20lda	20lda	al8f9j	la8f9j	vm48a	vm48a	a8sh7	a8sh7
97dj2	97dj2	m7foa	m7foa	ama39	ama93	29a26	29a26

Look at the four pairs of alpha-numerical digits. Circle or highlight the combination pair that **does not** match.

Sheet 4

w038f	w038f	e03ld4	e03ld4	lam48	lma48	a0lsn	a0lsn
28fj53	28fj53	0ld73h	0ld73h	amb58	amb58	rj39d	rg39d
38rsiw	38rsiw	d7i3bd	d73ibd	27dh3	27dh3	2e20d	2e20d
q2oe0	q20e0	k926ai	k926ai	n9j23	n9j23	fe0k2	fe0k2
dalpfn	dalpfn	ask348	ask348	qwplam	qwplam	29alpa	29alpa
fdmla	fdmla	347ash	347ahs	amw28	amw28	se19d	es19d
3f9am	3f9am	da37fh	da37fh	29dj20	29dj20	v9s6w	v9s6w
mda20	mad20	hs8j02	hs8j02	lp18jd	lpi8jd	l29aq	l29aq
249ame	249mae	rel29a	rel29a	498fao	498fao	ja93h3	ja93h3
ppo8ye	ppo8ye	al20r8	al20r8	23amrt	23mart	28snma	28snma
9euige	9euige	vbgu4	vbgu4	tra92m	tra92m	sm28ag	sm2a8g
cdn385	cdn385	49gjra	49gira	am20d	am20d	fdmla2	fdmla2
gh47sl	gh47sl	348gfj	348gfj	39fja0	39fja0	1e27rt	1e27rt
sk38rp	sk83rp	29en2	29en2	1047f	1047f	0gle79	ogle79
d83hfe	d83hfe	208fm	208fm	37659	37569	tr8fl3e	tr8fl3e
39lp82	39lp82	opww7	opwu7	m8c62	m8c62	c93ma	c93ma
l2a74	i2a74	38fk19	38fk19	wp39sl	wp39sl	34927	34927
itu38d	itu38d	193753	193573	lsmc37	lscm37	lpqun	lpqun
bmdk2	bmdk2	e9r8t6	e9r8t6	dh37ql	dh37ql	frn37	frn37
am38d	am38d	l9689w	l9689w	io16ah	io16ah	29do3	29d03
398daj	398daj	w93mc	w93mc	cm39al	cm39al	h92jd6	h92jd6
10ripa	10rlpa	ep28a	ep82a	al28rua	al28ura	29s1la	29s1la
amd21	amd21	0ql173	0ql173	e382f0	e382f0	a81l03	8a1l03
p08j7a	p08j7a	2479a	2479a	fek381	fek381	936el2	936el2
gh38sk	gh38sk	x3d6g8	x3d6g8	xmsl37	xsml37	bb37dka	bb37kda
29sl28	29sl28	0nmf6s	0nmf6s	2846fw	2846fw	vm389fe	vm389fe
s6g9j0	s9g6j0	6bf93m	6fb93m	m97gd6	m97gd6	lfdh38g	lfdh38g
v745n2	v745n2	dk291n	dk291n	dh28q8	dh28q8	dsj3476	dsj3476

*Look at the four pairs of alpha-numerical digits. Circle or highlight the combination pair that **does not** match.*

Sheet 5

389am2	389am2	jfjs238	jfjs238	3895fj	3895fj	a5h8f5	a5h8f5
20d86g	208d6g	39475	39475	ek28a	ek28a	me17eb	me17eb
cmd76	cmd76	397da	397da	pef28l	pel28f	me18eo	me18eo
r9846d	r9846d	24dj98	24jd98	fcn38	fcn38	st176a	st167a
van8s7	van8s7	vma7f9	vma7f9	348f37	348f37	mv83ah	mv38ah
xbos7z	xbox7z	fj37ara	fj37ara	29dm2	22dm9	dka18a	dka18a
qpal7fe	qpal7fe	0mv7fh	0mv7bh	18sn26	18sn26	pl8mfra	pl8mfra
e8mwa	e8mwa	hsd38a	hsd38a	2348hl	2348hl	aor237	aor237
na84	na84	awu38	awu38	8976f	8966f	y5f8h	y5f8h
ld72	ld72	bc894	bc894	768kl	768kl	0nh8f	0nh8f
29fg	29fg	387fh	387hf	58d3t	58d3t	d8gs2	dogs2
mcw6	mc26	29752	29752	t7ki0	t7ki0	58dv8	58dv8
vnd7l	vnd7l	nc7ek4	nc7ek4	nc63	nc63	2579	2579
0k76s	0k76s	gh30al	hg30al	2378	2378	dajp	dajp
me28a	me28e	cm20gf	cm20gf	piwr	piwr	394h	349h
ple8ah	ple8ah	s8pm2a	s8pm2a	fa8g	fag8	rqo2	rqo2
h83dk0	h38dk0	mc30g	mc30g	n7924	n7924	7420f	7420f
289hfa	289hfa	g4bh8	g4bh8	7420a	7402a	fsjfr3	fsjrf3
294875	294875	ry93t	ry93t	fjal3o	fjal3o	3573g	3573g
5389fs	5389fs	7539h	75e9h	r239a	r239a	c3b8g	c3b8g
chg84j	cha84j	kl926s	kl962s	qpri58	qpri58	cm349f	cm349f
dj38sg	dj38sg	djk27h	djk27h	39fpl3	39flp3	295fh7	259fh7
fkc823	fkc823	2749d0	2749d0	3k6bn	3k6bn	537dn3	537dn3
2846dh	2846dh	xdj278	xdj278	s9wn7	s9wn7	385792	385792
lsk389	lsk389	eilw18a	eilw18a	q8fm4n	q8fm4n	ldj72h	idj72h
38eb35	38be35	al4rnm	al4rnm	sm28da	sm82da	afkr3k	afkr3k
63ma98	63ma98	zcwr39	zcwr39	0kc3h8	0kc3h8	td9nm	td9nm
mcd3l0	mcd3l0	dal53nj	dai53nj	fh38ka	fh38ka	ud308t	ud308t

Look at the four pairs of alpha-numerical digits. Circle or highlight the combination pair that **does not** match.

Sheet 6

387aj3	387ja3	a5f8hk	a5f8hk	tuwopa	tuwopa	e82kfr	e82kfr
l037dg	l037dg	m56n3	m56n3	2084al	2484al	gvvn5	gavn5
kla73n	kla73n	lfm4ea	lm4ea	skfhj47	skfhj47	308fka	308fka
dm38a	dm38a	mrk48e	mrk48e	vkfh7c	vkfh7c	pal7fm	pal7fm

49an56	94an56	nv0f78	nv0f78	boot8a	boat8a	xmcl38	xmcl38
239pl3	239pl3	sl54j9	sl5499	rmnn5l	rmnn5l	qwok5o	qwko5o
3457r8	3457r8	mi5a82	mi5a82	alprmy	alprmy	m5nhjc	m5nhjc
2cm79r	2cm79r	akr308	akr308	30586	30586	h5820a	h5820a

938728	938278	emc84h	emc84h
953jf05	953jf05	03ldj63	03ldj63
po398a	po398a	qlpe28	qlpe28
vb39ala	vb39ala	xcpoi24	xcpol24

ANSWERS TO *TEST 3*

Sheet 1

dl49f dl49f	39dj5 39dj5	ep395 ep395	elp59 elp59
30f3r 30f3r	qp294 qp294	eptiy petiy	jkow8 jkow8
lo3vr lo3yr	doi39 doi39	39ri3 39ri3	do03r do03r
or35k or35k	d034i d034l	k5o58 k5o58	mlg94 mlg49

move3 move3	39fjw 39fjw	35957 35957	wp20e wp20e
yijn5 yijn5	pyk5k ypk5k	vmpw3 vmpw3	fmog4 fmog4
fkp30 fk3p0	fmv93 fmv93	deok5 deok5	vmpeg mvpeg
deklp deklp	dmp24 dmp24	rpk60 rpk06	204dk 204dk

ri40e ri40e	fjo39 fjo93	wpa10 wpa01	fejmo fejmo
or30r or30r	powe2 powe2	dld93 dld93	308jo 308jo
fk04j fk04j	dk035 dk035	dkv92 dkv92	r30ie r30ie
t40gj t04gj	358fj 358fj	s024k s024k	20oew 20eow

395kr 395kr	fem34 fem34	09668 09668	trjo3 trjo3
mcl39 mci39	dkp30 dkp30	jig7t jij7t	lpeea lpeaa
jlgt0 jlgt0	20dmv 2odmv	o9ubj o9ubj	f3k63 f3k63
r04ir r04ir	dkf30 dkf30	k0i76 k0i76	fpk46 fpk46

tk303 tk303	gfo3k5 gfo3k5	35fe3 35fe3	lr39fp lr39fp
rlpf2 rlfp2	59eu3 59ue3	350dk 350kd	flp30 flp03
flp3d flp3d	34oiro 34oiro	q130e q130e	fro46 fro46
dkp20 dkp20	3058d 3058d	vmlt3 vmlt3	t4240 t4240

gml45 gml45	dwo14 dwo14	35erp 53erp	3fjo3p 3fjo3p
340rk 340rk	304or 304ro	wp24r wp24r	eoo42 eoo42
e2l04 e2i04	092lp 092lp	fm40e fm40e	mv3o4 mv34o
r3k05 r3k05	2dwp2 2dwp2	emp53 emp53	kop94 kop94

f46ju f46ju	roi3q roi3p	aklq9u1 aklq9u1	35fap1 35fpa1
ssu9s ssu9s	249dj 249dj	dkpc96 dkpc96	dl304r dl304r
skp97 skp97	djo07 djo07	bkpw08 bkpw08	cmp29 cmp29
mo906 mo960	hoit7 hoit7	n08dpp no8dpp	rkp30 rkp30

Sheet 2

fdsp2	fdsp2	eok35	eko35	adp53	adp53	aoj53	aoj53
sa245	sa245	dkwp3	dkwp3	sdlp4	sdlp4	vmpt4	vmpt4
dfvm4	dfvm4	wek46	wek46	fnk3k	fnk3k	repk3	repk3
w563g	w536g	kp57d	kp57d	aslk5	asl5k	dwl53	dwi53
5r9t4	5r9t4	359fj	359fj	qk4kg	gk4kg	grkl3	grkl3
grkp4	grkp4	aru95	aru95	fmlfe4	fmlfe4	frk3r	frkr3
gfm35	gfn35	ryy85	ryy85	tkp40	tkp40	vmlf9	vmlf9
dl35jt	dl35jt	a9u47	a9u74	40irjw	40irjw	dpl69	dpl69
fek42	fek42	gh39a	gh39a	the93	the93	g349fn	g349fn
wij3n	wij3n	amm6f	amm6f	tpe38r	tpe38r	fel48r	fel48r
tmp46	tmp46	flk64	fik64	mfep4	mfep4	twnl3	townl3
m35ja	m35ga	polk5	polk5	r39fe	r93fe	rjow3	rjow3
grtlm4	grtlm4	g9345	g9345	euiorw	eiuorw	35992	35992
bvm3r	bvm3r	38702	38702	wero35	wero35	fnsk3	fns23
5jre30	5lre30	etnkd	entkd	gf35ir	gf35ir	39nr3	39nr3
35793	35793	34098	34098	nro3nr	nro3nr	em6l7	em6l7
gfn4nt	gfn4nt	68753	68753	xdkl4	xdkj4	kjhfy	kjhfy
rm3l2	rm321	freojr	freoir	zprli	zprli	hui96	hui96
yml34	yml34	vcmne	vcmne	itu38	itu38	oj97g	0j97g
plghi3	plghi3	35089	35089	nml30	nml30	nlk9t	nlk9t
kgy7f	kgy7f	gdkn4	gdkn4	campt3	campt3	fajioj	fajioj
987jl	987jli	fejio5	fejio5	dfsfm6	dfsfm6	wplai	wplai
mb905	mb905	plhih8	plhih8	gjasp5	gjsap5	caaop	caaop
cyt86r	cyt86r	nkr39	nrk39	hsk64	hsk64	oarji	oarjil
35983	35983	yaok5	yaok5	29082	29028	fla35a	fla35a
20957	60957	iimpy7	iimpy7	qpalfm	qpalfm	al38gh	al38gh
247d9	247d9	gkdpm	gkdmp	mcao4	mcao4	daml46	dami46
ae3k4	ae3k4	3598j	3598j	nb39f	nb39f	faml57	faml57

Sheet 3

03ke3 03ke3	d63ju d63ju	sal35k sal53k	30irwk 30irwk
xmcl9 xmci9	qpel29 qpel29	oiu48a oiu48a	ewpe2 wepe2
e3lmr e3lmr	drlp35 drlp35	m38ak m38ak	wwekp wwekp
46lgm 46lgm	nfl3pq nfl3qp	as29sk as29sk	2394e 2394e
3580ak 358oak	salp3 salp3	salpt salpt	cxa4l3 cxa4l3
dasl53 dasl53	rel86 rel86	gdko4 gdko4	l23lr5 l32lr5
adkl34 adkl34	ro35j ro35g	39dj3 39dj3	tlep4k tlep4k
gdlok5 gdlok5	lpsa2 lpsa2	vek2k vekk2	rk4kar rk4kar
3lp5g 3lp5g	w29di w29dd	sal238 sal238	etplgf etpglf
ktgr4 ktgr4	dsko3 dsko3	249716 294716	grmo4 grmo4
5l3j2 5l3i2	hspl2 hspl2	aso2kr aso2kr	trmeo trmeo
a90fg a90fg	k120d k120d	rek3ko rek3ko	3048d 3048d
uialpa uialpa	cemuv cemuv	yafm4l yafm4l	49738 94738
apslfm paslfm	eokwa eokwa	49frj3 49frj3	42980 42980
dskape dskape	s2le0e s2leeo	0ds2j ods2j	asjoe asjoe
oial30 oial30	lp30a lp30a	198dw 198dw	dsok2 dsok2
bnr3if bnr3if	rei301 rei031	a9dt4 a9dt4	93jd1 93jd1
x20ala x20ala	aspl11 aspl11	4m6l7 4m6i7	10sk2 10ks2
z19al6 z19al6	pyt94a pyt94a	ly4pd ly4pd	ek20p ek20p
q204ld g204ld	idsjwa idsjwa	d3u9r d3u9r	y02jr y02jr
s92md s92md	694fk 694fk	ou92m ou92m	29ap2k 29ap2k
d19am d19am	e2i01 e2i01	mc92a mc92a	dsk2a9 ds2ka9
wpqa0 wpqao	cm30a mc30a	nap29 nap92	ma02la ma02la
prm28 prm28	kao2a kao2a	ka17s ka17s	a9dk39 a9dk39
k29ak k29ak	45da7 45da7	op08a op08a	28ak9 28ak9
7al20 7ai20	92mf2 92mf2	a7rn5 a7rn5	19sk1 19ks1
20lda 20lda	al8f9j la8f9j	vm48a vm48a	a8sh7 a8sh7
97dj2 97dj2	m7foa m7foa	ama39 ama93	29a26 29a26

Sheet 4

w038f w038f	e03ld4 e03ld4	lam48 lma48	a0lsn a0lsn	
28fj53 28fj53	0ld73h 0ld73h	amb58 amb58	rj39d rg39d	
38rsiw 38rsiw	d7i3bd d73ibd	27dh3 27dh3	2e20d 2e20d	
q2oe0 q20e0	k926ai k926ai	n9j23 n9j23	fe0k2 fe0k2	

dalpfn dalpfn	ask348 ask348	qwplam qwplam	29alpa 29alpa
fdmla fdmla	347ash 347ahs	amw28 amw28	se19d es19d
3f9am 3f9am	da37fh da37fh	29dj20 29dj20	v9s6w v9s6w
mda20 mad20	hs8j02 hs8j02	lp18jd lpi8jd	l29aq l29aq

249ame 249mae	rel29a rel29a	498fao 498fao	ja93h3 ja93h3
ppo8ye ppo8ye	al20r8 al20r8	23amrt 23mart	28snma 28snma
9euige 9euige	vbgu4 vbgu4	tra92m tra92m	sm28ag sm2a8g
cdn385 cdn385	49gjra 49gira	am20d am20d	fdmla2 fdmla2

gh47sl gh47sl	348gfj 348gfj	39fja0 39fja0	1e27rt 1e27rt
sk38rp sk83rp	29en2 29en2	1047f 1047f	0gle79 ogle79
d83hfe d83hfe	208fm 208fm	37659 37569	tr8fl3e tr8fl3e
39lp82 39lp82	opww7 opwu7	m8c62 m8c62	c93ma c93ma

l2a74 i2a74	38fk19 38fk19	wp39sl wp39sl	34927 34927
itu38d itu38d	193753 193573	lsmc37 lscm37	lpqun lpqun
bmdk2 bmdk2	e9r8t6 e9r8t6	dh37ql dh37ql	frn37 frn37
am38d am38d	l9689w l9689w	io16ah io16ah	29do3 29d03

398daj 398daj	w93mc w93mc	cm39al cm39al	h92jd6 h92jd6
10ripa 10rlpa	ep28a ep82a	al28rua al28ura	29s1la 29s1la
amd21 amd21	0ql173 0ql173	e382f0 e382f0	a81l03 8a1l03
p08j7a p08j7a	2479a 2479a	fek381 fek381	936el2 936el2

gh38sk gh38sk	x3d6g8 x3d6g8	xmsl37 xsml37	bb37dka bb37kda
29sl28 29sl28	0nmf6s 0nmf6s	2846fw 2846fw	vm389fe vm389fe
s6g9j0 s9g6j0	6bf93m 6fb93m	m97gd6 m97gd6	lfdh38g lfdh38g
v745n2 v745n2	dk291n dk291n	dh28q8 dh28q8	dsj3476 dsj3476

Sheet 5

389am2	389am2	jfjs238	jfjs238	3895fj	3895fj	a5h8f5	a5h8f5
20d86g	208d6g	39475	39475	ek28a	ek28a	me17eb	me17eb
cmd76	cmd76	397da	397da	pef28l	pel28f	me18eo	me18eo
r9846d	r9846d	24dj98	24jd98	fcn38	fcn38	st176a	st167a

van8s7	van8s7	vma7f9	vma7f9	348f37	348f37	mv83ah	mv38ah
xbos7z	xbox7z	fj37ara	fj37ara	29dm2	22dm9	dka18a	dka18a
qpal7fe	qpal7fe	0mv7fh	0mv7bh	18sn26	18sn26	pl8mfra	pl8mfra
e8mwa	e8mwa	hsd38a	hsd38a	2348hl	2348hl	aor237	aor237

na84	na84	awu38	awu38	8976f	8966f	y5f8h	y5f8h
ld72	ld72	bc894	bc894	768kl	768kl	0nh8f	0nh8f
29fg	29fg	387fh	387hf	58d3t	58d3t	d8gs2	dogs2
mcw6	mc26	29752	29752	t7ki0	t7ki0	58dv8	58dv8

vnd7l	vnd7l	nc7ek4	nc7ek4	nc63	nc63	2579	2579
0k76s	0k76s	gh30al	hg30al	2378	2378	dajp	dajp
me28a	me28e	cm20gf	cm20gf	piwr	piwr	394h	349h
ple8ah	ple8ah	s8pm2a	s8pm2a	fa8g	fag8	rqo2	rqo2

h83dk0	h38dk0	mc30g	mc30g	n7924	n7924	7420f	7420f
289hfa	289hfa	g4bh8	g4bh8	7420a	7402a	fsjfr3	fsjrf3
294875	294875	ry93t	ry93t	fjal3o	fjal3o	3573g	3573g
5389fs	5389fs	7539h	75e9h	r239a	r239a	c3b8g	c3b8g

chg84j	cha84j	kl926s	kl962s	qpri58	qpri58	cm349f	cm349f
dj38sg	dj38sg	djk27h	djk27h	39fpl3	39flp3	295fh7	259fh7
fkc823	fkc823	2749d0	2749d0	3k6bn	3k6bn	537dn3	537dn3
2846dh	2846dh	xdj278	xdj278	s9wn7	s9wn7	385792	385792

lsk389	lsk389	eilw18a	eilw18a	q8fm4n	q8fm4n	ldj72h	idj72h
38eb35	38be35	al4rnm	al4rnm	sm28da	sm82da	afkr3k	afkr3k
63ma98	63ma98	zcwr39	zcwr39	0kc3h8	0kc3h8	td9nm	td9nm
mcd3l0	mcd3l0	dal53nj	dai53nj	fh38ka	fh38ka	ud308t	ud308t

Sheet 6

387aj3	387ja3	a5f8hk	a5f8hk	tuwopa	tuwopa	e82kfr	e82kfr
l037dg	l037dg	m56n3	m56n3	2084al	2484al	gvvn5	gavn5
kla73n	kla73n	lfm4ea	lm4ea	skfhj47	skfhj47	308fka	308fka
dm38a	dm38a	mrk48e	mrk48e	vkfh7c	vkfh7c	pal7fm	pal7fm

49an56	94an56	nv0f78	nv0f78	boot8a	boat8a	xmcl38	xmcl38
239pl3	239pl3	sl54j9	sl5499	rmnn5l	rmnn5l	qwok5o	qwko5o
3457r8	3457r8	mi5a82	mi5a82	alprmy	alprmy	m5nhjc	m5nhjc
2cm79r	2cm79r	akr308	akr308	30586	30586	h5820a	h5820a

938728	938278	emc84h	emc84h
953jf05	953jf05	03ldj63	03ldj63
po398a	po398a	qlpe28	qlpe28
vb39ala	vb39ala	xcpoi24	xcpol24

TEST 4

(Alpha-Numerical Comparison)

(You will be given **150 questions** which should be completed using the time limit of **5 minutes**).

Look at the four pairs of alpha-numerical digits. Circle or highlight the combination pair that **does not** match.

Sheet 1

la0s	la0s	w5f8	w5f8	e6t9	e6t9	a8fm	8afm
a0d8	aod8	7mw2	7mw2	74b2	742b	47rb	47rb
48fm	48fm	das3	das3	046f	046f	v7sa	v7sa
s7f5	s7f5	935f	953f	0od8	0od8	9gdm	9gdm
d5h8	d5h8	r6i0	r6l0	gh78	gh78	ed58	ed58
m9b7	m9b7	0md3	0md3	hj9f	hj9f	9ki6	9kl6
git7	git7	35f7	35f7	6897	6987	76hi	76hi
79g7	76g7	y4ma	y4ma	gu72	gu72	458y	458y
d76h	d76h	df7h	df7h	w2r5	w2r5	t8y3	toy3
g8i9	g8i9	8yhg	8yhg	o0u7	o0u7	mc32	mc32
78yt	78yt	7t03	7to3	y5y7	y57y	5378	5378
87yj	87yg	nc4f	nc4f	ty38	ty38	ru93	ru93
dajk	dajk	de0k	de0k	q34i	q34i	67dk	67dk
353a	353a	87yu	87uy	m8d4	m8d4	k907	k907
su89	su89	9uit	9uit	f87o	f870	7689	7869
35jf	35if	6r98	6r98	ghi6	ghi6	v68j	v68j
ryi9	ryi9	3e46	3a46	m9g6	m9j6	mce8	mce8
wert	wetr	f8hk	f8hk	wfr8	wfr8	g4j9	g4l9
mnbv	mnbv	bn8f	bn8f	i764	i764	248f	248f
c678	c678	df94	df94	oiu7	oiu7	539a	539a
5rg8	5rg8	t7i9	t7i9	z69m	z69m	e5i9	e5i9
tj85	tj85	r6gh	r6gh	z6ag	z6ag	lo90	io90
hdd2	hdd2	kju6	kuj6	an8o	an8o	r7yu	r7yu
sam2	san2	g7hf	g7hf	m964	m694	n8y5	n8y5
e5u8	e5u8	rt8y	rt8j	fj49	fi49	ul19	ul91
l0j7	l0j7	hhfd	hhfd	cm39	cm39	o486	o486
g7k0	g7k0	asdn	asdn	th92	th92	dm37	dm37
mv7u	mu7u	rj38	rj38	akld	akld	vmd7	vmd7

*Look at the four pairs of alpha-numerical digits. Circle or highlight the combination pair that **does not** match.*

Sheet 2

mv83 mv83	f3h8 f3h8	qopl qopl	la9r la9r
gj3j gj3j	c3m9 cm39	w348 w348	39ey 39ye
so28 s028	2508 2508	vma2 vma2	w925 w925
ajk3 ajk3	8yud 8yud	397f 937f	vnb3 vnb3

2745 2745	5237 5327	ka85 ka85	e2o0 e2o0
apru apru	daj9 daj9	j85a g85a	i9e7 i97e
gvm7 gum7	r3u9 r3u9	fa56 fa56	yt47 yt47
eh37 eh37	iuy7 iuy7	zb75 zb75	t472 t472

nfr7 nfr7	t4u8 t4v8	eo28 eo28	ooeu ooeu
r382 r482	f3j9 f3j9	298e 298e	3857 3587
q947 q947	2395 2395	cma6 cma6	fdk9 fdk9
mfdh mfdh	v9vm v9vm	m705 n705	4358 4358

m86f m86f	kjs8 kis8	lap8 lap8	p9l7 p9l7
578j 578i	sjf7 sjf7	r38a r38a	i8yu i8uy
5e8h 5e8h	3rn6 3rn6	2349 2349	t5e3 t5e3
g853 g853	63n3 63n3	v39a v93a	na6a na6a

th38 th38	q760 q760	r6i9 r6i9	cb37 cb37
dfjk dfik	l975 l975	m8f5 m8f5	e38f e38f
32e2 32e2	ej3n ej3m	sd56 sd65	t3m6 t3m6
q3w0 q3w0	4m37 4m37	i974 i974	69g6 69g9

qp29 qp29	e29c e29c	a6d9 a6d9	qt70 qt70
gm5b gmb5	38f7 38f7	04m6 04n6	m389 m389
s7ch s7ch	4m67 4n67	5n59 5n59	38yf 38yf
5mg7 5mg7	2b5m 2b5m	5n38 5n38	398j 389j

r4t7 r4t7	u8t6 u8t6	s4y8 s4y8	pl8a pl8a
lu9t lu9t	u895 u895	8hjl 8hjl	aj85 ay85
y487 x487	678u 678v	f6ih f6ih	a576 a576
488t 488t	iuy6 iuy6	r68g r68j	g789 g789

Look at the four pairs of alpha-numerical digits. Circle or highlight the combination pair that **does not** match.

Sheet 3

f6yu8	f6yu8	ar69k	ar69k	lo87t	lo87t	ft5ei	ft5ei
h875r	h875r	mia7s	mia7s	dj8d6	dj8d6	tro54	tro54
j9m76	jm976	su89d	su89d	cmcr3	cmcr3	bv8sd	bvosd
d5tr8	d5tr8	cu86s	cu68s	ru38a	ru83a	sr8g5	sr8g5

t39tj	t93tj	d6h9b	d6h9b	78yut	78yut	um7b6	um7b6
4j47f	4j47f	28sju	28sju	4r7y4	4r7u4	6n5v4	6n5v4
r47f9	r47f9	2n46k	2n46k	9hj4b	9hj4b	5g8je	5g8ej
h8f5a	h8f5a	7nm53	7mn53	4mg8a	4mg8a	y834d	y834d

8m76h	8m76h	y47fj	y47fj	fdi39	fdl39	asm36	ams36
45f79	45f79	4d76h	4a76h	34ryt	34ryt	48ty4	48ty4
juu89	juu89	pal78	pal78	459ir	459ir	t483g	t483g
a58ha	a5h8a	vm57f	vm57f	456ua	456ua	hu459	hu459

jfi47	jfi47	3478r	3478r	bb7e4	bb7e4	85mf7	85mf7
g48v7	g48v7	39ik0	39ik0	nj3b8	nj3b8	4jkf7	4jkf7
y40kh	y40hk	y58h8	y85h8	48gm4	48mg4	d04mf	d04mf
389m3	389m3	hg4o0	hg4o0	27d0t	27d0t	sl48k	si48k

4jfs0	4fjs0	e6th9	e6th9	gl59m	gl95m	a2f5h	a2f5h
m6s74	m6s74	383m7	388m7	t89s6	t89s6	m56f4	n56f4
fkt84	fkt84	m3x85	m3x85	fm40f	fm40f	lf39g	lf39g
gtk38	gtk38	s6ns7	s6ns7	49r3y	49r3y	t4i0t	t4i0t

56gf3	56gf3	ry4n8	ry4n8	n8d64	n8d64	48t07	48t07
78jg4	78j4g	g94hf	g94hf	d6g9h	d6g9h	334m9	334n9
67htg	67htg	fdm8g	fmd8g	5mf73	5mf37	64n36	64n36
mju5s	mju5s	g93jf	g93jf	b85oh	b85oh	348a7	348a7

7vd5m	7vd5m	6g9j3	6g9j3	vm49f	vm49f	3578p	3578p
y8s54	y8s54	3edy4	3edu4	fu93k	fu93k	49it4	49it4
h9r7s	h9r7s	48tj0	48tj0	af378	af738	64u88	49ti4
g7as5	glas5	426f6	426f6	cu9r3	cu9r3	r4y73	r4y73

Look at the four pairs of alpha-numerical digits. Circle or highlight the combination pair that **does not** match.

Sheet 4

37r3y	37r3y	t49fn	t49fn	6d03m	6d03m	us9gf	us9gf
3c957	3d957	3bvj6	3bvj6	38cve	38cve	gkg83	gkg83
loda7	loda7	gn7s6	gn76s	e93jr	e93jr	39f8k	39f8k
va84g	va84g	6na68	6na68	yi5j2	yl5j2	648dg	648gd

21674	21674	e69jl	e69jl	53g05	53g05	a5f8h	a5f8h
truip	truip	d845b	d845b	496s4	469s4	7m5b3	7m5b3
gfhjk	gjhjk	h836a	h386a	50hk7	50hk7	g84d5	g48d5
vcmbn	vcmbn	am3n5	am3n5	7j5g6	7j5g6	7nt4r	7nt4r

e2u9f	e2v9f	mbn48	mbn48	k7b5x	k7b5x	g7hj0	g7hjo
0hm6b	0hm6b	t49rv	t49rv	zv4b5	zv4b5	n5b27	n5b27
4b8f4	4b8f4	rhf97	rhf97	q6g8h	q9g8h	fgh83	fgh83
79hk5	79hk5	fj9b5	fy9b5	dk9g6	dk9g6	v0p3l	v0p3l

k7h56	k7h56	t7kim	t7kim	26db0	26db0	7n9tf	7n9tf
g6df8	g6fd8	96g90	96g90	034nf	o34nf	97nkd	97nkd
k96bs	k96bs	mk9de	m9kde	93ms5	93ms5	8ch3k	8ch3k
j97tv	j97tv	2f6j9	2f6j9	92m3c	92m3c	3nm53	3mn53

s37g9	s37g9	v8m78	v8m78	64b0l	64bol	24748	24748
9uj64	9uj64	6g3a7	6g3a7	6tjgf	6tjgf	8753f	8753f
7gjn3	7gyn3	987k8	978k8	954df	954df	086g3	086g3
9mxr6	9mxr6	742u0	742u0	f456k	f456k	53ky5	53yk5

7m5v3	7m5v3	589j5	589j5	86h94	86h94	g8k96	g89k6
9nm4s	9nm4s	ekn74	ekn74	866d4	866d4	86hj9	86hj9
9y3df	9u3df	hmj95	hmy95	i9g64	i9g46	d6bj6	d6bj6
64h6n	64h6n	nkl76	nkl76	8j5d5	8j5d5	9jne4	9jne4

87g5d	87g5d	08m5s	08m5s	0kl7h	0kl7h	a5d8h	a5d8h
9j7d3	9j7d3	85b84	8b584	6b4s3	6b43s	n9f75	n97f5
e5bg8	eb5g8	mvc8j	mvc8j	86hi8	86hi8	s7fg4	s7fg4
j9y5e	j9y5e	m974d	m974d	095f8	095f8	49gw4	49gw4

Look at the four pairs of alpha-numerical digits. Circle or highlight the combination pair that **does not** match.

Sheet 5

d8gn27	d8gn27	fy378m	fy378m	a8dm58	a8dm58	d73kf9	d73kf9
plday3	plday3	397d4a	397d4a	dlr75c	dlr75c	0l3f6h	0l3f6h
4g8j6g	4g8j6g	0m7g54	om7g54	97548c	97548c	6dg8dj	6gd8dj
3d760j	3e760j	8dkb7a	8dkb7a	cm38bs	mc38bs	s5f8hm	s5f8hm
a4d7c9	a4d7c9	q6r8m5	q6r8m5	h75f7k	h75f7k	s539gm	s539gm
ldjk73	ldjk73	gm94nb	gm94nb	k96bhd	k69bhd	03r8g4	03r8g4
395gj5	395gi5	v894ml	v894ml	5d9ghr	5d9ghr	r37h8t	r37h8t
e945kr	e945kr	hk04ny	hk04yn	mv84nf	mv84nf	4nmvg3	4mnvg3
vgf740	vgf740	q478tk	q478tk	74mc8j	74mc8j	q438k6	q438k6
39it3y	39it3y	034m5n	033m5n	fdj4nfd	fdj4nfd	pl58gn	pi58gn
r380i4	r380j4	64n49t	64n49t	83h8d2	83hd82	uin85n	uin85n
ad9j3f	ad9j3f	36f9m8	36f9m8	03lu4a	03lu4a	yun68f	yun68f
9k7h6d	9k76hd	e3j6mt	e3j6mt	f6j9k7	f6j9k7	q6u80o	q6u80o
378f94	378f94	94mpg7	94mgp7	mn79kl	mn79kl	m76h5d	m76h5d
48hjg4	48hjg4	g94bgu	g94bgu	eh97k0	eh97k0	39gdj8	39adj8
akamto	akamto	g9gouy	g9gouy	l074gh	l704gh	97hkid	97hkid
l98hf6	l98hf6	56jkn7	56jkn7	w4u9km	w4uk9m	i86t8o	i86t8o
ung74f	ung74f	974df7	974df7	kh78ok	kh78ok	oi6fh8	o6ifh8
0m7n5d	0n7n5d	9kyer6	9kjer6	m64257	m64257	mk75gf	mk75gf
97f48j	97f48j	9634md	9634md	864h90	864h90	jkuu36	jkuu36
ty84gh	ty84gh	m85t79i	m85t79i	r68kna	r68kna	965yu9	965yu9
o986nk	o986nk	kg34gh	kg34gh	ld7cn6	ld7cn6	ui85e4	ui85e4
k976fj	k976fj	uy6rfv	uy6rfv	9e6sn2	96esn2	49ug47	49gu47
876rhn	876hrn	qpla8f	pqla8f	679ed8	679ed8	97nu64	97nu64
08u75g	08u75g	t669j6	t669j6	468hf5	468hf5	124q79	214q79
86h5f7	86h5f7	j865g6	j865g6	8uin64	8uin64	875h85	875h85
98mf57	98m5f7	l905f6	l905f6	23jd78	23dj78	7u5d8o	7u5d8o
i975gj	i975gj	854f7h	845f7h	69jka4	69jka4	8654de	8654de

Look at the four pairs of alpha-numerical digits. Circle or highlight the combination pair that **does not** match.

Sheet 6

348g4	348g4	4eds8	4eds8	285fh	285fh	357hf8	357hf8
t348a	t438a	9jh46	9jh46	34jf3	34jf3	83f3g7	83t3g7
84k5f	84k5f	3738f	7338f	9jfa6	9jfa6	jg8497	jg8497
93ja5	93ja5	3bm6f	3bm6f	mc367	mc637	3hf6k3	3hf6k3

qy79jf	qy79jf	83mf9p	83mf9p	t4da	t4da	328a7	328a7
dd7aya	dd7aya	348tu7	348tu7	faj7	faj7	ut4o5	ut405
04mv74	04mv74	3y7t39	3u7t39	64g7	64g7	du84m	du84m
r84jf9	r84fj9	93may7	93may7	46a3	64a3	4g7m8	4g7m8

3mc7h	3mc7h	q6g9m	q6g9m	q7mg7	q7mg7	zm8ch	zmc8h
48g0k	48g0k	f7d6g	f7dog	c8hf6	c8hf6	xm7f5	xm7f5
5g9a6	5g9a6	39g53	39g53	jk7f6	yk7f6	3nc84	3nc84
n79v7	n97v7	vm96h	vm96h	f8j4g	f8j4g	f85n8	f85n8

ANSWERS TO *TEST 4*

Sheet 1

la0s	la0s	w5f8	w5f8	e6t9	e6t9	a8fm	8afm
a0d8	aod8	7mw2	7mw2	74b2	742b	47rb	47rb
48fm	48fm	das3	das3	046f	046f	v7sa	v7sa
s7f5	s7f5	935f	953f	0od8	0od8	9gdm	9gdm
d5h8	d5h8	r6i0	r6l0	gh78	gh78	ed58	ed58
m9b7	m9b7	0md3	0md3	hj9f	hj9f	9ki6	9kl6
git7	git7	35f7	35f7	6897	6987	76hi	76hi
79g7	76g7	y4ma	y4ma	gu72	gu72	458y	458y
d76h	d76h	df7h	df7h	w2r5	w2r5	t8y3	toy3
g8i9	g8i9	8yhg	8yhg	o0u7	o0u7	mc32	mc32
78yt	78yt	7t03	7to3	y5y7	y57y	5378	5378
87yj	87yg	nc4f	nc4f	ty38	ty38	ru93	ru93
dajk	dajk	de0k	de0k	q34i	q34i	67dk	67dk
353a	353a	87yu	87uy	m8d4	m8d4	k907	k907
su89	su89	9uit	9uit	f87o	f870	7689	7869
35jf	35if	6r98	6r98	ghi6	ghi6	v68j	v68j
ryi9	ryi9	3e46	3a46	m9g6	m9j6	mce8	mce8
wert	wetr	f8hk	f8hk	wfr8	wfr8	g4j9	g4l9
mnbv	mnbv	bn8f	bn8f	i764	i764	248f	248f
c678	c678	df94	df94	oiu7	oiu7	539a	539a
5rg8	5rg8	t7i9	t7i9	z69m	z69m	e5i9	e5i9
tj85	tj85	r6gh	r6gh	z6ag	z6ag	lo90	io90
hdd2	hdd2	kju6	kuj6	an8o	an8o	r7yu	r7yu
sam2	san2	g7hf	g7hf	m964	m694	n8y5	n8y5
e5u8	e5u8	rt8y	rt8j	fj49	fi49	ul19	ul91
l0j7	l0j7	hhfd	hhfd	cm39	cm39	o486	o486
g7k0	g7k0	asdn	asdn	th92	th92	dm37	dm37
mv7u	mu7u	rj38	rj38	akld	akld	vmd7	vmd7

Sheet 2

mv83	mv83	f3h8	f3h8	qopl	qopl	la9r	la9r
gj3j	gj3j	c3m9	cm39	w348	w348	39ey	39ye
so28	s028	2508	2508	vma2	vma2	w925	w925
ajk3	ajk3	8yud	8yud	397f	937f	vnb3	vnb3
2745	2745	5237	5327	ka85	ka85	e2o0	e2o0
apru	apru	daj9	daj9	j85a	g85a	i9e7	i97e
gvm7	gum7	r3u9	r3u9	fa56	fa56	yt47	yt47
eh37	eh37	iuy7	iuy7	zb75	zb75	t472	t472
nfr7	nfr7	t4u8	t4v8	eo28	eo28	ooeu	ooeu
r382	r482	f3j9	f3j9	298e	298e	3857	3587
q947	q947	2395	2395	cma6	cma6	fdk9	fdk9
mfdh	mfdh	v9vm	v9vm	m705	n705	4358	4358
m86f	m86f	kjs8	kis8	lap8	lap8	p9l7	p9l7
578j	578i	sjf7	sjf7	r38a	r38a	i8yu	i8uy
5e8h	5e8h	3rn6	3rn6	2349	2349	t5e3	t5e3
g853	g853	63n3	63n3	v39a	v93a	na6a	na6a
th38	th38	q760	q760	r6i9	r6i9	cb37	cb37
dfjk	dfik	l975	l975	m8f5	m8f5	e38f	e38f
32e2	32e2	ej3n	ej3m	sd56	sd65	t3m6	t3m6
q3w0	q3w0	4m37	4m37	i974	i974	69g6	69g9
qp29	qp29	e29c	e29c	a6d9	a6d9	qt70	qt70
gm5b	gmb5	38f7	38f7	04m6	04n6	m389	m389
s7ch	s7ch	4m67	4n67	5n59	5n59	38yf	38yf
5mg7	5mg7	2b5m	2b5m	5n38	5n38	398j	389j
r4t7	r4t7	u8t6	u8t6	s4y8	s4y8	pl8a	pl8a
lu9t	lu9t	u895	u895	8hjl	8hjl	aj85	ay85
y487	x487	678u	678v	f6ih	f6ih	a576	a576
488t	488t	iuy6	iuy6	r68g	r68j	g789	g789

Sheet 3

f6yu8 f6yu8	ar69k ar69k	lo87t lo87t	ft5ei ft5ei
h875r h875r	mia7s mia7s	dj8d6 dj8d6	tro54 tro54
j9m76 jm976	su89d su89d	cmcr3 cmcr3	bv8sd bvosd
d5tr8 d5tr8	cu86s cu68s	ru38a ru83a	sr8g5 sr8g5
t39tj t93tj	d6h9b d6h9b	78yut 78yut	um7b6 um7b6
4j47f 4j47f	28sju 28sju	4r7y4 4r7u4	6n5v4 6n5v4
r47f9 r47f9	2n46k 2n46k	9hj4b 9hj4b	5g8je 5g8ej
h8f5a h8f5a	7nm53 7mn53	4mg8a 4mg8a	y834d y834d
8m76h 8m76h	y47fj y47fj	fdi39 fdl39	asm36 ams36
45f79 45f79	4d76h 4a76h	34ryt 34ryt	48ty4 48ty4
juu89 juu89	pal78 pal78	459ir 459ir	t483g t483g
a58ha a5h8a	vm57f vm57f	456ua 456ua	hu459 hu459
jfi47 jfi47	3478r 3478r	bb7e4 bb7e4	85mf7 85mf7
g48v7 g48v7	39ik0 39ik0	nj3b8 nj3b8	4jkf7 4jkf7
y40kh y40hk	y58h8 y85h8	48gm4 48mg4	d04mf d04mf
389m3 389m3	hg4o0 hg4o0	27d0t 27d0t	sl48k si48k
4jfs0 4fjs0	e6th9 e6th9	gl59m gl95m	a2f5h a2f5h
m6s74 m6s74	383m7 388m7	t89s6 t89s6	m56f4 n56f4
fkt84 fkt84	m3x85 m3x85	fm40f fm40f	lf39g lf39g
gtk38 gtk38	s6ns7 s6ns7	49r3y 49r3y	t4i0t t4i0t
56gf3 56gf3	ry4n8 ry4n8	n8d64 n8d64	48t07 48t07
78jg4 78j4g	g94hf g94hf	d6g9h d6g9h	334m9 334n9
67htg 67htg	fdm8g fmd8g	5mf73 5mf37	64n36 64n36
mju5s mju5s	g93jf g93jf	b85oh b85oh	348a7 348a7
7vd5m 7vd5m	6g9j3 6g9j3	vm49f vm49f	3578p 3578p
y8s54 y8s54	3edy4 3edu4	fu93k fu93k	49it4 49it4
h9r7s h9r7s	48tj0 48tj0	af378 af738	64u88 49ti4
g7as5 glas5	426f6 426f6	cu9r3 cu9r3	r4y73 r4y73

Sheet 4

37r3y 37r3y 3c957 3d957 loda7 loda7 va84g va84g	t49fn t49fn 3bvj6 3bvj6 gn7s6 gn76s 6na68 6na68	6d03m 6d03m 38cve 38cve e93jr e93jr yi5j2 yl5j2	us9gf us9gf gkg83 gkg83 39f8k 39f8k 648dg 648gd
21674 21674 truip truip gfhjk gjhjk vcmbn vcmbn	e69jl e69jl d845b d845b h836a h386a am3n5 am3n5	53g05 53g05 496s4 469s4 50hk7 50hk7 7j5g6 7j5g6	a5f8h a5f8h 7m5b3 7m5b3 g84d5 g48d5 7nt4r 7nt4r
e2u9f e2v9f 0hm6b 0hm6b 4b8f4 4b8f4 79hk5 79hk5	mbn48 mbn48 t49rv t49rv rhf97 rhf97 fj9b5 fy9b5	k7b5x k7b5x zv4b5 zv4b5 q6g8h q9g8h dk9g6 dk9g6	g7hj0 g7hjo n5b27 n5b27 fgh83 fgh83 v0p3l v0p3l
k7h56 k7h56 g6df8 g6fd8 k96bs k96bs j97tv j97tv	t7kim t7kim 96g90 96g90 mk9de m9kde 2f6j9 2f6j9	26db0 26db0 034nf o34nf 93ms5 93ms5 92m3c 92m3c	7n9tf 7n9tf 97nkd 97nkd 8ch3k 8ch3k 3nm53 3mn53
s37g9 s37g9 9uj64 9uj64 7gjn3 7gyn3 9mxr6 9mxr6	v8m78 v8m78 6g3a7 6g3a7 987k8 978k8 742u0 742u0	64b0l 64bol 6tjgf 6tjgf 954df 954df f456k f456k	24748 24748 8753f 8753f 086g3 086g3 53ky5 53yk5
7m5v3 7m5v3 9nm4s 9nm4s 9y3df 9u3df 64h6n 64h6n	589j5 589j5 ekn74 ekn74 hmj95 hmy95 nkl76 nkl76	86h94 86h94 866d4 866d4 i9g64 i9g46 8j5d5 8j5d5	g8k96 g89k6 86hj9 86hj9 d6bj6 d6bj6 9jne4 9jne4
87g5d 87g5d 9j7d3 9j7d3 e5bg8 eb5g8 j9y5e j9y5e	08m5s 08m5s 85b84 8b584 mvc8j mvc8j m974d m974d	0kl7h 0kl7h 6b4s3 6b43s 86hi8 86hi8 095f8 095f8	a5d8h a5d8h n9f75 n97f5 s7fg4 s7fg4 49gw4 49gw4

Sheet 5

d8gn27	d8gn27	fy378m	fy378m	a8dm58	a8dm58	d73kf9	d73kf9
plday3	plday3	397d4a	397d4a	dlr75c	dlr75c	0l3f6h	0l3f6h
4g8j6g	4g8j6g	0m7g54	om7g54	97548c	97548c	6dg8dj	6gd8dj
3d760j	3e760j	8dkb7a	8dkb7a	cm38bs	mc38bs	s5f8hm	s5f8hm

a4d7c9	a4d7c9	q6r8m5	q6r8m5	h75f7k	h75f7k	s539gm	s539gm
ldjk73	ldjk73	gm94nb	gm94nb	k96bhd	k69bhd	03r8g4	03r8g4
395gj5	395gi5	v894ml	v894ml	5d9ghr	5d9ghr	r37h8t	r37h8t
e945kr	e945kr	hk04ny	hk04yn	mv84nf	mv84nf	4nmvg3	4mnvg3

vgf740	vgf740	q478tk	q478tk	74mc8j	74mc8j	q438k6	q438k6
39it3y	39it3y	034m5n	033m5n	fdj4nfd	fdj4nfd	pl58gn	pi58gn
r380i4	r380j4	64n49t	64n49t	83h8d2	83hd82	uin85n	uin85n
ad9j3f	ad9j3f	36f9m8	36f9m8	03lu4a	03lu4a	yun68f	yun68f

9k7h6d	9k76hd	e3j6mt	e3j6mt	f6j9k7	f6j9k7	q6u80o	q6u80o
378f94	378f94	94mpg7	94mgp7	mn79kl	mn79kl	m76h5d	m76h5d
48hjg4	48hjg4	g94bgu	g94bgu	eh97k0	eh97k0	39gdj8	39adj8
akamto	akamto	g9gouy	g9gouy	l074gh	l704gh	97hkid	97hkid

l98hf6	l98hf6	56jkn7	56jkn7	w4u9km	w4uk9m	i86t8o	i86t8o
ung74f	ung74f	974df7	974df7	kh78ok	kh78ok	oi6fh8	o6ifh8
0m7n5d	0n7n5d	9kyer6	9kjer6	m64257	m64257	mk75gf	mk75gf
97f48j	97f48j	9634md	9634md	864h90	864h90	jkuu36	jkuu36

ty84gh	ty84gh	m85t79i	m85t79i	r68kna	r68kna	965yu9	965yu9
o986nk	o986nk	kg34gh	kg34gh	ld7cn6	ld7cn6	ui85e4	ui85e4
k976fj	k976fj	uy6rfv	uy6rfv	9e6sn2	96esn2	49ug47	49gu47
876rhn	876hrn	qpla8f	pqla8f	679ed8	679ed8	97nu64	97nu64

08u75g	08u75g	t669j6	t669j6	468hf5	468hf5	124q79	214q79
86h5f7	86h5f7	j865g6	j865g6	8uin64	8uin64	875h85	875h85
98mf57	98m5f7	l905f6	l905f6	23jd78	23dj78	7u5d8o	7u5d8o
i975gj	i975gj	854f7h	845f7h	69jka4	69jka4	8654de	8654de

Sheet 6

348g4 348g4	4eds8 4eds8	285fh 285fh	357hf8 357hf8
t348a t438a	9jh46 9jh46	34jf3 34jf3	83f3g7 83t3g7
84k5f 84k5f	3738f 7338f	9jfa6 9jfa6	jg8497 jg8497
93ja5 93ja5	3bm6f 3bm6f	mc367 mc637	3hf6k3 3hf6k3
qy79jf qy79jf	83mf9p 83mf9p	t4da t4da	328a7 328a7
dd7aya dd7aya	348tu7 348tu7	faj7 faj7	ut4o5 ut4o5
04mv74 04mv74	3y7t39 3u7t39	64g7 64g7	du84m du84m
r84jf9 r84fj9	93may7 93may7	46a3 64a3	4g7m8 4g7m8
3mc7h 3mc7h	q6g9m q6g9m	q7mg7 q7mg7	zm8ch zmc8h
48g0k 48g0k	f7d6g f7dog	c8hf6 c8hf6	xm7f5 xm7f5
5g9a6 5g9a6	39g53 39g53	jk7f6 yk7f6	3nc84 3nc84
n79v7 n97v7	vm96h vm96h	f8j4g f8j4g	f85n8 f85n8

TEST 5

(Numerical Comparison)

(You will be given **150 questions** which should be completed using the time limit of **5 minutes**).

*Look at the four pairs of numerical digits. Circle or highlight the combination pair that **does not** match.*

Sheet 1

938-917 938-917	452-417 452-417	058-174 058-174	497-961 497-961
178-815 178-815	148-163 148-163	287-427 287-247	104-952 140-952
193-131 193-113	964-642 964-642	248-186 248-186	745-438 745-438
410-137 410-137	427-246 472-246	193-164 193-164	258-735 258-735
749-556 749-556	160-035 160-035	794-795 974-795	416-494 416-494
336-464 336-464	064-635 064-635	135-579 135-579	795-920 795-920
564-759 546-759	790-164 790-164	146-905 146-905	113-792 113-792
795-295 795-295	136-498 136-489	354-561 354-561	194-795 149-795
497-795 497-795	264-561 264-561	716-405 716-405	794-792 794-792
792-715 729-715	176-792 176-792	298-594 298-594	678-792 678-792
120-097 120-097	126-045 126-045	146-460 146-460	284-684 234-684
791-496 791-496	015-461 051-461	166-790 166-970	283-278 283-278
791-425 791-425	578-364 578-364	756-479 756-279	465-796 465-796
284-462 284-462	963-416 963-416	963-741 963-741	548-514 548-154
689-861 689-861	324-464 324-446	201-064 201-064	636-464 636-464
167-462 167-642	269-561 269-561	097-971 097-971	438-462 438-462
497-456 497-456	547-962 574-962	369-461 369-461	764-462 746-462
369-410 369-410	632-102 632-102	316-421 316-421	269-798 269-798
468-790 486-790	367-461 367-461	048-751 048-751	467-461 467-461
308-710 308-710	795-405 795-405	187-461 187-641	168-840 168-840
795-450 795-450	465-795 465-795	019-735 109-735	069-479 069-479
369-796 369-796	397-725 397-725	369-705 369-705	479-791 479-971
167-461 167-461	497-796 947-796	068-462 068-462	567-795 567-795
169-789 169-987	398-894 398-894	568-784 568-784	029-741 029-741
029-791 029-791	458-769 458-769	460-462 406-462	634-497 634-497
497-952 497-952	899-675 899-657	569-894 569-894	894-795 894-795
367-861 367-891	597-746 597-746	794-562 794-562	569-713 569-731
456-795 456-795	369-795 369-795	297-541 297-541	638-745 638-745

*Look at the four pairs of numerical digits. Circle or highlight the combination pair that **does not** match.*

Sheet 2

79-8645 79-8645	69-7895 69-7895	47-8945 47-8945	97-9856 97-9856
63-7459 63-7459	21-4587 21-4578	72-4259 72-4529	48-7958 48-7958
15-8652 15-8562	63-8956 63-8956	36-7198 36-7198	39-7849 93-7849
21-4510 21-4510	58-7963 58-7963	91-7932 91-7932	92-2648 92-2648

47-8564 47-8564	78-7926 78-7962	49-7621 49-7621	78-8954 87-8954
36-7155 36-7155	36-8541 36-8541	96-7951 96-7951	96-9715 96-9715
59-7951 59-7915	15-9578 15-9578	16-4692 19-4692	23-5647 23-5647
02-5631 02-5631	10-2057 10-2057	25-4761 25-4761	10-2504 10-2504

78-8953 78-8953	45-8965 54-8965	15-9657 15-9657	35-9874 35-9874
23-6478 23-6478	57-4561 57-4561	96-9745 99-9745	36-4761 36-4716
02-3620 02-6320	36-5475 36-5475	28-7894 28-7894	18-6946 18-6946
04-9018 04-9018	15-7951 15-7951	25-8974 25-8974	27-5861 27-5861

58-7769 58-7769	79-7952 79-7952	96-8423 96-8423	48-8654 84-8654
36-7615 36-7615	02-8944 20-8944	42-7615 42-7615	25-9645 25-9645
26-7651 26-7650	10-7106 10-7106	05-9846 05-9846	27-1456 27-1456
56-7954 56-7954	07-5610 07-5610	93-8442 93-8842	12-6479 12-6479

74-8964 74-8964	78-8545 88-8545	74-5245 74-5245	47-9954 47-9954
25-9648 25-9648	36-6104 36-6104	69-4610 69-4601	68-4105 68-4105
10-7145 10-7415	36-7105 36-7105	35-8941 35-8941	46-4617 46-4617
03-8964 03-8964	39-8412 39-8412	25-6514 25-6514	57-9451 75-9451

97-7944 97-7944	49-7921 49-7921	79-6465 79-6465	02-4754 02-4754
26-4764 62-4764	15-7469 15-7469	15-6954 15-6594	36-7914 36-7914
12-4560 12-4560	09-7761 90-7761	23-3654 23-3654	42-7924 42-7924
08-4604 08-4604	45-9654 45-9654	26-4561 26-4561	97-4612 79-4612

75-8696 75-8696	74-9624 74-9624	09-7446 90-7446	40-9642 04-9642
36-4614 36-4614	36-8642 36-8642	71-4604 71-4604	48-7620 48-7620
97-6447 97-6647	15-7614 51-7614	25-5954 25-5954	46-9781 46-9781
92-0579 92-0579	09-4761 09-4761	52-8942 52-8942	09-8645 09-8645

*Look at the four pairs of numerical digits. Circle or highlight the combination pair that **does not** match.*

Sheet 3

79-746 79-746	19-762 19-762	79-761 79-761	79-936 79-936
16-795 16-795	79-864 79-846	29-476 29-476	36-460 36-460
39-746 93-746	44-564 44-564	16-441 16-411	08-719 08-719
24-461 24-461	26-764 26-764	15-704 15-704	09-764 09-746

08-923 80-923	19-078 19-087	09-746 07-746	15-984 15-984
05-464 05-464	13-085 13-085	04-975 04-975	25-674 25-674
85-510 85-510	63-941 63-941	64-547 64-547	96-971 96-970
96-714 96-714	10-164 10-164	95-841 95-841	25-546 25-546

98-725 98-725	75-936 75-936	09-761 09-661	96-745 96-745
69-059 69-059	36-154 36-154	75-915 75-915	15-964 15-964
23-647 23-647	36-542 36-544	39-954 39-954	25-875 25-875
09-446 90-446	74-951 74-951	05-361 05-361	95-190 95-109

48-965 48-965	08-974 08-974	09-735 90-735	74-952 74-952
68-951 68-915	96-872 96-872	62-715 62-715	70-308 70-308
14-766 14-766	36-056 36-506	60-100 60-100	79-059 79-059
04-936 04-936	04-647 04-647	06-691 06-691	76-535 67-535

74-561 74-561	09-791 09-791	47-947 47-947	79-485 76-485
69-789 69-789	96-495 96-495	54-421 54-421	29-864 29-864
02-918 02-918	56-795 56-795	05-647 05-647	59-764 59-764
57-460 57-640	24-971 24-917	63-058 63-958	15-465 15-465

47-465 47-456	58-746 58-746	47-564 47-564	74-856 74-856
09-765 09-765	69-851 69-851	69-846 69-846	96-423 66-423
08-345 08-345	05-945 05-945	39-764 93-764	09-974 09-974
94-761 94-761	45-746 55-746	06-647 06-647	49-764 49-764

78-864 78-864	48-964 48-964	49-764 49-764	47-964 41-964
86-641 86-641	69-761 69-761	69-886 69-886	69-864 69-864
59-461 59-461	26-456 26-456	69-696 69-669	05-476 05-476
37-649 73-649	58-942 85-942	96-745 96-745	59-994 59-994

*Look at the four pairs of numerical digits. Circle or highlight the combination pair that **does not** match.*

Sheet 4

36-476 36-476	45-791 45-791	49-765 49-765	96-461 96-461
26-464 26-464	36-642 36-642	02-765 02-765	09-674 09-674
14-791 14-791	50-761 50-761	29-567 92-567	09-641 06-641
36-464 63-464	68-897 88-897	08-756 08-756	58-641 58-641

79-644 79-644	95-791 95-791	58-964 58-964	97-876 97-876
69-764 96-764	29-764 29-764	75-643 75-643	75-621 57-621
09-476 09-476	15-894 15-894	29-735 29-735	36-458 36-458
48-674 48-674	29-764 29-746	39-671 39-677	12-457 12-457

25-369 25-369	85-746 85-746	47-856 47-856	75-965 57-965
59-754 59-754	69-854 69-854	98-745 89-745	15-467 15-467
20-954 20-954	25-645 25-645	25-157 25-157	69-410 69-410
23-974 32-974	67-108 67-180	06-910 06-910	05-756 05-756

96-751 96-751	96-741 96-741	96-745 69-745	58-658 56-658
25-964 25-964	25-357 25-357	25-965 25-965	74-635 74-635
36-542 63-542	12-362 12-362	42-354 42-354	25-671 25-671
12-015 12-015	05-753 50-753	23-410 23-410	05-843 05-843

85-742 85-724	65-428 65-428	58-558 58-558	15-360 15-360
06-581 06-581	36-985 63-985	66-616 66-661	12-745 12-745
03-050 03-050	25-194 25-194	96-689 96-689	63-452 63-852
04-587 04-587	48-508 48-508	69-668 69-668	74-064 74-064

69-854 69-854	59-684 59-684	48-692 48-692	78-100 78-100
36-452 36-542	26-405 26-405	36-521 36-521	02-254 02-254
10-936 10-936	63-804 36-804	05-486 05-846	36-460 36-460
09-753 09-753	75-904 75-904	06-752 06-752	89-461 98-461

85-965 85-965	78-645 78-465	75-995 57-995	58-964 58-964
39-461 39-461	09-754 09-754	98-845 98-845	48-571 48-571
06-461 09-461	69-751 69-751	26-475 26-475	36-520 36-520
79-478 79-478	25-706 25-706	36-257 36-257	24-227 24-272

*Look at the four pairs of numerical digits. Circle or highlight the combination pair that **does not** match.*

Sheet 5

1-7954 1-7954	7-8974 7-8974	4-7923 4-7923	5-7986 5-7989
5-7984 5-7984	3-6442 3-6444	0-4647 0-4647	3-5647 3-5647
6-7897 6-7987	5-5476 5-5476	0-9665 0-9695	2-9796 2-9796
6-7641 6-7641	3-4561 3-4561	6-4567 6-4567	2-9861 2-9861

4-7956 4-7956	0-8976 0-8967	5-6345 5-6345	9-7941 9-7941
3-6797 3-7697	6-9759 6-9759	3-5647 3-5647	8-7972 8-7973
3-6741 3-6741	7-6494 7-6494	9-9971 9-9671	2-5647 2-5647
0-8944 0-8944	5-9796 5-9796	2-6919 2-6919	2-6972 2-6972

5-9479 5-9479	7-9792 7-9792	4-7953 4-7953	4-9479 4-9479
6-7972 6-7972	3-9472 3-9472	3-4978 1-4978	3-5697 3-5697
5-9785 6-9785	6-7941 6-7941	6-9721 6-9721	2-9448 2-9948
8-9715 8-9715	2-5647 2-6547	0-8947 0-8947	6-5642 6-5642

7-4576 7-4576	8-7946 9-7946	4-9476 4-9276	5-5647 5-5647
5-9725 5-9725	3-4567 3-4567	3-9417 3-9417	2-9497 2-9497
2-6472 2-6742	5-6941 5-6941	2-9647 2-9647	2-4672 2-4972
1-9715 1-9715	2-9657 2-9657	0-5694 0-5694	0-5678 0-5678

7-5694 7-5694	7-4794 7-4794	4-7945 4-7945	9-6647 9-6647
5-5972 5-5972	2-7943 2-7493	2-4678 2-4678	7-7915 7-7951
3-6471 3-6471	3-4647 3-4647	0-2698 0-2698	6-9752 6-9752
0-2647 0-2947	6-5892 6-5892	6-4972 9-4972	5-6512 5-6512

8-8947 8-8947	0-5976 0-5976	9-7895 9-7895	9-7953 9-7953
3-4564 3-4564	3-4975 3-4975	3-6497 3-6497	3-6497 3-4697
2-5647 2-5467	2-8775 2-8715	3-1028 3-0128	6-7915 6-7915
6-6791 6-6791	3-6549 3-6549	4-0974 4-0974	2-5894 2-5894

7-4792 7-4792	4-1264 4-1264	7-7946 7-7946	7-7715 7-7175
6-7895 6-7895	6-5497 6-5497	9-5974 9-5974	6-6448 6-6448
2-8954 2-8954	3-6914 3-6941	5-5597 5-5597	6-9641 6-9641
6-5614 6-6514	0-5947 0-5947	6-6698 6-6968	2-6971 2-6971

*Look at the four pairs of numerical digits. Circle or highlight the combination pair that **does not** match.*

Sheet 6

594-564 594-564	587-652 587-652	758-674 758-674	759-697 579-697
798-461 798-461	369-415 369-415	364-715 364-715	126-064 126-064
134-764 134-674	254-731 254-731	675-642 755-642	047-560 047-560
369-741 369-741	059-350 509-350	375-651 375-651	370-460 370-460

589-751 589-751	859-854 859-584	475-698 475-698	065-149 065-149
239-764 239-746	698-654 698-654	365-541 635-541	302-087 302-087
298-543 298-543	268-354 268-354	297-354 297-354	350-597 350-597
279-764 279-764	368-379 368-379	297-461 297-461	389-587 839-587

796-358 799-358	497-765 497-765
369-475 369-475	394-764 934-764
348-189 348-189	597-761 597-761
167-098 167-098	375-154 375-154

ANSWERS TO *TEST 5*

Sheet 1

938-917 938-917	452-417 452-417	058-174 058-174	497-961 497-961
178-815 178-815	148-163 148-163	287-427 287-247	104-952 140-952
193-131 193-113	964-642 964-642	248-186 248-186	745-438 745-438
410-137 410-137	427-246 472-246	193-164 193-164	258-735 258-735
749-556 749-556	160-035 160-035	794-795 974-795	416-494 416-494
336-464 336-464	064-635 064-635	135-579 135-579	795-920 795-920
564-759 546-759	790-164 790-164	146-905 146-905	113-792 113-792
795-295 795-295	136-498 136-489	354-561 354-561	194-795 149-795
497-795 497-795	264-561 264-561	716-405 716-405	794-792 794-792
792-715 729-715	176-792 176-792	298-594 298-594	678-792 678-792
120-097 120-097	126-045 126-045	146-460 146-460	284-684 234-684
791-496 791-496	015-461 051-461	166-790 166-970	283-278 283-278
791-425 791-425	578-364 578-364	756-479 756-279	465-796 465-796
284-462 284-462	963-416 963-416	963-741 963-741	548-514 548-154
689-861 689-861	324-464 324-446	201-064 201-064	636-464 636-464
167-462 167-642	269-561 269-561	097-971 097-971	438-462 438-462
497-456 497-456	547-962 574-962	369-461 369-461	764-462 746-462
369-410 369-410	632-102 632-102	316-421 316-421	269-798 269-798
468-790 486-790	367-461 367-461	048-751 048-751	467-461 467-461
308-710 308-710	795-405 795-405	187-461 187-641	168-840 168-840
795-450 795-450	465-795 465-795	019-735 109-735	069-479 069-479
369-796 369-796	397-725 397-725	369-705 369-705	479-791 479-971
167-461 167-461	497-796 947-796	068-462 068-462	567-795 567-795
169-789 169-987	398-894 398-894	568-784 568-784	029-741 029-741
029-791 029-791	458-769 458-769	460-462 406-462	634-497 634-497
497-952 497-952	899-675 899-657	569-894 569-894	894-795 894-795
367-861 367-891	597-746 597-746	794-562 794-562	569-713 569-731
456-795 456-795	369-795 369-795	297-541 297-541	638-745 638-745

Sheet 2

79-8645	79-8645	69-7895	69-7895	47-8945	47-8945	97-9856	97-9856
63-7459	63-7459	21-4587	21-4578	72-4259	72-4529	48-7958	48-7958
15-8652	15-8562	63-8956	63-8956	36-7198	36-7198	39-7849	93-7849
21-4510	21-4510	58-7963	58-7963	91-7932	91-7932	92-2648	92-2648
47-8564	47-8564	78-7926	78-7962	49-7621	49-7621	78-8954	87-8954
36-7155	36-7155	36-8541	36-8541	96-7951	96-7951	96-9715	96-9715
59-7951	59-7915	15-9578	15-9578	16-4692	19-4692	23-5647	23-5647
02-5631	02-5631	10-2057	10-2057	25-4761	25-4761	10-2504	10-2504
78-8953	78-8953	45-8965	54-8965	15-9657	15-9657	35-9874	35-9874
23-6478	23-6478	57-4561	57-4561	96-9745	99-9745	36-4761	36-4716
02-3620	02-6320	36-5475	36-5475	28-7894	28-7894	18-6946	18-6946
04-9018	04-9018	15-7951	15-7951	25-8974	25-8974	27-5861	27-5861
58-7769	58-7769	79-7952	79-7952	96-8423	96-8423	48-8654	84-8654
36-7615	36-7615	02-8944	20-8944	42-7615	42-7615	25-9645	25-9645
26-7651	26-7650	10-7106	10-7106	05-9846	05-9846	27-1456	27-1456
56-7954	56-7954	07-5610	07-5610	93-8442	93-8842	12-6479	12-6479
74-8964	74-8964	78-8545	88-8545	74-5245	74-5245	47-9954	47-9954
25-9648	25-9648	36-6104	36-6104	69-4610	69-4601	68-4105	68-4105
10-7145	10-7415	36-7105	36-7105	35-8941	35-8941	46-4617	46-4617
03-8964	03-8964	39-8412	39-8412	25-6514	25-6514	57-9451	75-9451
97-7944	97-7944	49-7921	49-7921	79-6465	79-6465	02-4754	02-4754
26-4764	62-4764	15-7469	15-7469	15-6954	15-6594	36-7914	36-7914
12-4560	12-4560	09-7761	90-7761	23-3654	23-3654	42-7924	42-7924
08-4604	08-4604	45-9654	45-9654	26-4561	26-4561	97-4612	79-4612
75-8696	75-8696	74-9624	74-9624	09-7446	90-7446	40-9642	04-9642
36-4614	36-4614	36-8642	36-8642	71-4604	71-4604	48-7620	48-7620
97-6447	97-6647	15-7614	51-7614	25-5954	25-5954	46-9781	46-9781
92-0579	92-0579	09-4761	09-4761	52-8942	52-8942	09-8645	09-8645

Sheet 3

79-746 79-746	19-762 19-762	79-761 79-761	79-936 79-936
16-795 16-795	79-864 79-846	29-476 29-476	36-460 36-460
39-746 93-746	44-564 44-564	16-441 16-411	08-719 08-719
24-461 24-461	26-764 26-764	15-704 15-704	09-764 09-746
08-923 80-923	19-078 19-087	09-746 07-746	15-984 15-984
05-464 05-464	13-085 13-085	04-975 04-975	25-674 25-674
85-510 85-510	63-941 63-941	64-547 64-547	96-971 96-970
96-714 96-714	10-164 10-164	95-841 95-841	25-546 25-546
98-725 98-725	75-936 75-936	09-761 09-661	96-745 96-745
69-059 69-059	36-154 36-154	75-915 75-915	15-964 15-964
23-647 23-647	36-542 36-544	39-954 39-954	25-875 25-875
09-446 90-446	74-951 74-951	05-361 05-361	95-190 95-109
48-965 48-965	08-974 08-974	09-735 90-735	74-952 74-952
68-951 68-915	96-872 96-872	62-715 62-715	70-308 70-308
14-766 14-766	36-056 36-506	60-100 60-100	79-059 79-059
04-936 04-936	04-647 04-647	06-691 06-691	76-535 67-535
74-561 74-561	09-791 09-791	47-947 47-947	79-485 76-485
69-789 69-789	96-495 96-495	54-421 54-421	29-864 29-864
02-918 02-918	56-795 56-795	05-647 05-647	59-764 59-764
57-460 57-640	24-971 24-917	63-058 63-958	15-465 15-465
47-465 47-456	58-746 58-746	47-564 47-564	74-856 74-856
09-765 09-765	69-851 69-851	69-846 69-846	96-423 66-423
08-345 08-345	05-945 05-945	39-764 93-764	09-974 09-974
94-761 94-761	45-746 55-746	06-647 06-647	49-764 49-764
78-864 78-864	48-964 48-964	49-764 49-764	47-964 41-964
86-641 86-641	69-761 69-761	69-886 69-886	69-864 69-864
59-461 59-461	26-456 26-456	69-696 69-669	05-476 05-476
37-649 73-649	58-942 85-942	96-745 96-745	59-994 59-994

Sheet 4

36-476 36-476	45-791 45-791	49-765 49-765	96-461 96-461
26-464 26-464	36-642 36-642	02-765 02-765	09-674 09-674
14-791 14-791	50-761 50-761	29-567 92-567	09-641 06-641
36-464 63-464	68-897 88-897	08-756 08-756	58-641 58-641

79-644 79-644	95-791 95-791	58-964 58-964	97-876 97-876
69-764 96-764	29-764 29-764	75-643 75-643	75-621 57-621
09-476 09-476	15-894 15-894	29-735 29-735	36-458 36-458
48-674 48-674	29-764 29-746	39-671 39-677	12-457 12-457

25-369 25-369	85-746 85-746	47-856 47-856	75-965 57-965
59-754 59-754	69-854 69-854	98-745 89-745	15-467 15-467
20-954 20-954	25-645 25-645	25-157 25-157	69-410 69-410
23-974 32-974	67-108 67-180	06-910 06-910	05-756 05-756

96-751 96-751	96-741 96-741	96-745 69-745	58-658 56-658
25-964 25-964	25-357 25-357	25-965 25-965	74-635 74-635
36-542 63-542	12-362 12-362	42-354 42-354	25-671 25-671
12-015 12-015	05-753 50-753	23-410 23-410	05-843 05-843

85-742 85-724	65-428 65-428	58-558 58-558	15-360 15-360
06-581 06-581	36-985 63-985	66-616 66-661	12-745 12-745
03-050 03-050	25-194 25-194	96-689 96-689	63-452 63-852
04-587 04-587	48-508 48-508	69-668 69-668	74-064 74-064

69-854 69-854	59-684 59-684	48-692 48-692	78-100 78-100
36-452 36-542	26-405 26-405	36-521 36-521	02-254 02-254
10-936 10-936	63-804 36-804	05-486 05-846	36-460 36-460
09-753 09-753	75-904 75-904	06-752 06-752	89-461 98-461

85-965 85-965	78-645 78-465	75-995 57-995	58-964 58-964
39-461 39-461	09-754 09-754	98-845 98-845	48-571 48-571
06-461 09-461	69-751 69-751	26-475 26-475	36-520 36-520
79-478 79-478	25-706 25-706	36-257 36-257	24-227 24-272

Sheet 5

1-7954 1-7954	7-8974 7-8974	4-7923 4-7923	5-7986 5-7989
5-7984 5-7984	3-6442 3-6444	0-4647 0-4647	3-5647 3-5647
6-7897 6-7987	5-5476 5-5476	0-9665 0-9695	2-9796 2-9796
6-7641 6-7641	3-4561 3-4561	6-4567 6-4567	2-9861 2-9861

4-7956 4-7956	0-8976 0-8967	5-6345 5-6345	9-7941 9-7941
3-6797 3-7697	6-9759 6-9759	3-5647 3-5647	8-7972 8-7973
3-6741 3-6741	7-6494 7-6494	9-9971 9-9671	2-5647 2-5647
0-8944 0-8944	5-9796 5-9796	2-6919 2-6919	2-6972 2-6972

5-9479 5-9479	7-9792 7-9792	4-7953 4-7953	4-9479 4-9479
6-7972 6-7972	3-9472 3-9472	3-4978 1-4978	3-5697 3-5697
5-9785 6-9785	6-7941 6-7941	6-9721 6-9721	2-9448 2-9448
8-9715 8-9715	2-5647 2-6547	0-8947 0-8947	6-5642 6-5642

7-4576 7-4576	8-7946 9-7946	4-9476 4-9276	5-5647 5-5647
5-9725 5-9725	3-4567 3-4567	3-9417 3-9417	2-9497 2-9497
2-6472 2-6742	5-6941 5-6941	2-9647 2-9647	2-4672 2-4972
1-9715 1-9715	2-9657 2-9657	0-5694 0-5694	0-5678 0-5678

7-5694 7-5694	7-4794 7-4794	4-7945 4-7945	9-6647 9-6647
5-5972 5-5972	2-7943 2-7493	2-4678 2-4678	7-7915 7-7951
3-6471 3-6471	3-4647 3-4647	0-2698 0-2698	6-9752 6-9752
0-2647 0-2947	6-5892 6-5892	6-4972 9-4972	5-6512 5-6512

8-8947 8-8947	0-5976 0-5976	9-7895 9-7895	9-7953 9-7953
3-4564 3-4564	3-4975 3-4975	3-6497 3-6497	3-6497 3-4697
2-5647 2-5467	2-8775 2-8715	3-1028 3-0128	6-7915 6-7915
6-6791 6-6791	3-6549 3-6549	4-0974 4-0974	2-5894 2-5894

7-4792 7-4792	4-1264 4-1264	7-7946 7-7946	7-7715 7-7175
6-7895 6-7895	6-5497 6-5497	9-5974 9-5974	6-6448 6-6448
2-8954 2-8954	3-6914 3-6941	5-5597 5-5597	6-9641 6-9641
6-5614 6-6514	0-5947 0-5947	6-6698 6-6968	2-6971 2-6971

Sheet 6

594-564 594-564	587-652 587-652	758-674 758-674	759-697 579-697
798-461 798-461	369-415 369-415	364-715 364-715	126-064 126-064
134-764 134-674	254-731 254-731	675-642 755-642	047-560 047-560
369-741 369-741	059-350 509-350	375-651 375-651	370-460 370-460
589-751 589-751	859-854 859-584	475-698 475-698	065-149 065-149
239-764 239-746	698-654 698-654	365-541 635-541	302-087 302-087
298-543 298-543	268-354 268-354	297-354 297-354	350-597 350-597
279-764 279-764	368-379 368-379	297-461 297-461	389-587 839-587
796-358 799-358	497-765 497-765		
369-475 369-475	394-764 934-764		
348-189 348-189	597-761 597-761		
167-098 167-098	375-154 375-154		

TEST 6

(Numerical Comparison)

(You will be given **150 questions** which should be completed
using the time limit of **5 minutes**).

*Look at the four pairs of numerical digits. Circle or highlight the combination pair that **does not** match.*

Sheet 1

4795 4795	7986 7986	5976 5979	4976 4976
4597 4597	6985 6985	9678 9678	6985 6985
9597 5997	3654 3654	2047 2047	3298 3928
5894 5894	0167 1067	2345 2345	2497 2497
4978 4978	7958 7958	2957 2957	2594 2594
2975 2957	3974 3974	9856 9856	0197 0197
2978 2978	7946 7646	3964 3994	1957 1957
3989 3989	3982 3982	3985 3985	2671 2971
9876 9876	4972 4972	5975 5675	4972 4972
6985 9685	3368 3368	9674 9674	2236 2236
4598 4598	8869 8669	3648 3648	0164 0164
2948 2948	7569 7569	0954 0954	2010 2001
9759 9759	0947 0947	0947 0947	0914 9014
3697 3697	9464 9461	2397 2397	0975 0975
3694 3964	3795 3795	3370 3770	9803 9803
0914 0914	0972 0972	1043 1043	3048 3048
9053 9053	0594 0594	4176 4716	0951 0951
3067 3067	3997 3997	8964 8964	5013 5073
9975 9975	0984 0984	2369 2369	3049 3049
0659 6059	6669 6966	2697 2697	5809 5809
0894 0894	8079 8079	0814 0814	4982 4682
9765 9765	6874 6874	0716 0716	0846 0846
2397 2377	3654 3654	0069 0066	9876 9876
0956 0956	3097 3079	0076 0076	4535 4535
5986 5686	0556 0556	9507 9507	7965 7956
2647 2647	2694 2694	3310 3310	2987 2987
0849 0849	4920 4902	3641 3641	9875 9875
2970 2970	1697 1697	0671 0761	1897 1897

*Look at the four pairs of numerical digits. Circle or highlight the combination pair that **does not** match.*

Sheet 2

97565 97565	49756 49756	04965 04965	05946 05649
39545 39545	29880 27980	09809 09809	56781 56781
26405 26405	09876 09876	98704 98407	26486 26486
39544 34594	02564 02564	06497 06497	29778 29778
02564 02546	52981 52981	02945 02945	90575 90575
67954 67954	02947 02947	11657 11657	63187 63187
06975 06975	68974 68974	59874 59847	61709 61907
25987 25987	99843 98493	22687 22687	49781 49781
09597 09597	02947 02947	05944 05944	09807 09807
97461 97416	29746 29476	52971 52971	64782 64782
29754 29754	29771 29771	44985 99485	31597 31597
23578 23578	19784 19784	39574 39574	24567 24765
09564 90564	02569 02569	09597 09597	01694 01694
59714 59714	94615 94615	69786 69786	01623 01623
16078 16078	09544 90544	39897 39987	06221 06221
03124 03124	61613 61613	29784 29784	01562 01526
05915 05519	63987 63987	52946 54296	10064 10064
59574 59574	34965 34965	95789 95789	23548 24358
23647 23647	10097 01097	64130 64130	29040 29040
23564 23564	08946 08946	09753 09753	29841 29841
98595 98595	97873 97873	29087 29087	49795 49795
49775 49775	29871 29781	96745 96755	25977 27957
25998 25989	29840 29840	59754 59754	79516 79516
26487 26487	38956 38956	29878 29878	23948 23948
49762 49762	22222 22222	09594 09594	49598 49568
29874 29874	55555 55555	29873 29873	89846 89846
29829 28929	66666 66966	37956 93756	39774 39774
98795 98795	88888 88888	29671 29671	05478 05478

Look at the four pairs of numerical digits. Circle or highlight the combination pair that **does not** match.

Sheet 3

46954	46954	06978	06987	26548	26548	06597	06597
97955	97955	95467	95467	98710	08719	59975	57975
09878	09788	98840	98840	09814	09814	22997	22997
97815	97815	66478	66478	98578	98578	95754	95754
09594	09594	79742	97742	04926	04926	02954	02954
89799	89799	29759	29759	79561	79516	29875	29875
95641	95641	39775	39775	29753	29753	20497	20497
09875	90875	29788	29788	28782	28782	35694	53694
88759	88759	05977	05977	25569	25659	00698	00698
96754	96754	23971	23971	59746	59746	07985	07985
74026	74206	36981	36981	36978	36978	02547	20547
03697	03697	29478	92478	29087	29087	09804	09804
95876	95867	49876	49876	45984	45684	65987	65987
69569	69569	39857	93857	36952	36952	36542	36542
60945	60945	09587	09587	36978	36978	06589	06589
74598	74598	39496	39496	36540	36540	69896	66896
39878	39878	26487	26487	55597	55579	06955	06955
39854	39584	36985	36985	69856	69856	39878	39878
78952	78952	44958	44958	23147	23147	39547	39547
26870	26870	65885	65855	21352	21352	95252	92525
29546	29546	78594	78594	88759	87759	65985	65985
96856	96856	36654	36645	96658	96658	36547	36547
36475	39475	06659	06659	23265	23265	36202	36200
35985	35985	95368	95368	35574	35574	39854	39854
58946	58646	49545	49545	36985	36985	59778	59718
32998	32998	29542	23542	85454	85554	95135	95135
79564	79564	02695	02695	49524	49524	36495	36495
29854	29854	29647	29647	29548	29548	89651	89651

*Look at the four pairs of numerical digits. Circle or highlight the combination pair that **does not** match.*

Sheet 4

489575 489575	748596 478596	587458 587458	458759 458159
659564 659564	365689 365689	698954 698954	369851 369851
239543 239543	194587 194587	365897 365897	355978 355978
239502 239520	957629 957629	293547 263547	298534 298534

589658 589658	259687 259681	293548 293548	857496 857496
265647 266547	367951 367951	985674 985674	664594 664594
095534 095534	236459 236459	951743 957143	598789 598789
298750 298750	779658 779658	397894 397894	898778 897878

559875 559875	557893 557983	447953 447953	559865 556865
366984 366984	006254 006254	395884 395884	325487 325487
594785 954785	065580 065580	294989 294989	698547 698547
200156 200156	100657 100657	239547 239574	399854 399854

557896 557896	005269 005269	598745 598744	226589 226589
699874 999874	298598 298598	698635 698635	998456 998456
369852 369852	559874 559874	364478 364478	366479 633479
194597 194597	259334 529334	915875 915875	915874 915874

587595 857595	115697 115697	475896 475896	479658 479658
152637 152637	369856 369856	157565 157565	698984 698984
369851 369851	136589 136589	569841 569841	265987 265997
036596 036596	369854 366854	005965 055965	395024 395024

524632 524632	574965 574965	447958 447958	498756 498756
369857 369857	366989 366689	336985 336985	369854 369854
103355 013355	498956 498956	259535 259555	159753 519753
005098 005098	069578 069578	159787 159787	007589 007589

852369 852369	498785 498785	447859 447859	159683 159693
888695 888695	298533 298583	369545 369545	359687 359687
996696 996696	698547 698547	369852 369352	169598 169598
669869 699869	059423 059423	065895 065895	598632 598632

Look at the four pairs of numerical digits. Circle or highlight the combination pair that **does not** match.

Sheet 5

145664 145664	559865 559865	598654 568654	668597 668597
668859 668859	447859 447859	589631 589631	321596 321596
657495 567495	668563 668563	135986 135986	658714 658114
225698 225698	332569 382569	337489 337489	364587 364587
558754 588754	547856 547856	475825 475825	123658 123658
698653 698653	856472 856472	368541 368451	965413 965413
253659 253659	325698 325668	154875 154875	325987 395287
497846 497846	331456 331456	265987 265987	654986 654986
552699 552699	448554 448554	486698 486698	699335 699335
335984 335984	222598 222598	659545 569545	333639 333639
487596 487569	555525 555555	444445 444445	996369 996339
366521 366521	665466 665466	188746 188746	569654 569654
778549 778549	447896 447896	445887 445887	559986 559686
699552 699552	669856 669568	969658 969658	669853 669853
335433 335433	664875 664875	295484 295484	336657 336657
332656 332666	555819 555819	336694 366394	365998 365998
669894 669894	558954 558954	778965 778965	498765 498765
559878 559878	779562 775692	558745 554785	298865 298865
292487 292487	335965 335965	698983 698983	298562 298562
336479 339479	239878 239878	331597 331597	269774 269714
559898 559889	447586 447856	559686 559686	447856 487456
259584 259584	663257 663257	663896 663896	663256 663256
497887 497887	795859 795859	335987 335987	669954 669954
966254 966254	298584 298584	115141 115741	598791 598791
336659 336659	447589 447589	775985 775985	995875 995875
598787 598187	336985 336985	369854 639854	555857 555857
546559 546559	195856 195865	236948 236948	563594 593594
963648 963648	003651 003651	298745 298745	116985 116985

Look at the four pairs of numerical digits. Circle or highlight the combination pair that **does not** match.

Sheet 6

55986	55686	99658	99658	77485	77485	99685	99685
47989	47989	59788	59788	66958	69958	66547	66547
79859	79859	48515	48515	66935	66935	59865	59865
59878	59878	26897	29987	12358	12358	42164	41164

77859	77859	44785	44785	77498	77498	44989	44989
69895	69895	99658	99658	69983	69983	79865	79865
49874	49874	96631	96631	39965	39665	56123	56123
59835	95835	11305	11503	56989	56989	55535	55525

22235	22235	59365	59365	74985	74685	66958	66958
33358	33358	74989	47989	59955	59955	36995	36995
99969	96969	89632	89632	59878	59878	79465	74965
88878	88878	03619	03619	46132	46132	28944	28944

ANSWERS TO *TEST 6*

Sheet 1

4795 4795	7986 7986	5976 5979	4976 4976
4597 4597	6985 6985	9678 9678	6985 6985
9597 5997	3654 3654	2047 2047	3298 3928
5894 5894	0167 1067	2345 2345	2497 2497
4978 4978	7958 7958	2957 2957	2594 2594
2975 2957	3974 3974	9856 9856	0197 0197
2978 2978	7946 7646	3964 3994	1957 1957
3989 3989	3982 3982	3985 3985	2671 2971
9876 9876	4972 4972	5975 5675	4972 4972
6985 9685	3368 3368	9674 9674	2236 2236
4598 4598	8869 8669	3648 3648	0164 0164
2948 2948	7569 7569	0954 0954	2010 2001
9759 9759	0947 0947	0947 0947	0914 9014
3697 3697	9464 9461	2397 2397	0975 0975
3694 3964	3795 3795	3370 3770	9803 9803
0914 0914	0972 0972	1043 1043	3048 3048
9053 9053	0594 0594	4176 4716	0951 0951
3067 3067	3997 3997	8964 8964	5013 5073
9975 9975	0984 0984	2369 2369	3049 3049
0659 6059	6669 6966	2697 2697	5809 5809
0894 0894	8079 8079	0814 0814	4982 4682
9765 9765	6874 6874	0716 0716	0846 0846
2397 2377	3654 3654	0069 0066	9876 9876
0956 0956	3097 3079	0076 0076	4535 4535
5986 5686	0556 0556	9507 9507	7965 7956
2647 2647	2694 2694	3310 3310	2987 2987
0849 0849	4920 4902	3641 3641	9875 9875
2970 2970	1697 1697	0671 0761	1897 1897

Sheet 2

97565 97565	49756 49756	04965 04965	05946 05649
39545 39545	29880 27980	09809 09809	56781 56781
26405 26405	09876 09876	98704 98407	26486 26486
39544 34594	02564 02564	06497 06497	29778 29778
02564 02546	52981 52981	02945 02945	90575 90575
67954 67954	02947 02947	11657 11657	63187 63187
06975 06975	68974 68974	59874 59847	61709 61907
25987 25987	99843 98493	22687 22687	49781 49781
09597 09597	02947 02947	05944 05944	09807 09807
97461 97416	29746 29476	52971 52971	64782 64782
29754 29754	29771 29771	44985 99485	31597 31597
23578 23578	19784 19784	39574 39574	24567 24765
09564 90564	02569 02569	09597 09597	01694 01694
59714 59714	94615 94615	69786 69786	01623 01623
16078 16078	09544 90544	39897 39987	06221 06221
03124 03124	61613 61613	29784 29784	01562 01526
05915 05519	63987 63987	52946 54296	10064 10064
59574 59574	34965 34965	95789 95789	23548 24358
23647 23647	10097 01097	64130 64130	29040 29040
23564 23564	08946 08946	09753 09753	29841 29841
98595 98595	97873 97873	29087 29087	49795 49795
49775 49775	29871 29781	96745 96755	25977 27957
25998 25989	29840 29840	59754 59754	79516 79516
26487 26487	38956 38956	29878 29878	23948 23948
49762 49762	22222 22222	09594 09594	49598 49568
29874 29874	55555 55555	29873 29873	89846 89846
29829 28929	66666 66966	37956 93756	39774 39774
98795 98795	88888 88888	29671 29671	05478 05478

Sheet 3

46954	46954	06978	06987	26548	26548	06597	06597
97955	97955	95467	95467	98710	08719	59975	57975
09878	09788	98840	98840	09814	09814	22997	22997
97815	97815	66478	66478	98578	98578	95754	95754

09594	09594	79742	97742	04926	04926	02954	02954
89799	89799	29759	29759	79561	79516	29875	29875
95641	95641	39775	39775	29753	29753	20497	20497
09875	90875	29788	29788	28782	28782	35694	53694

88759	88759	05977	05977	25569	25659	00698	00698
96754	96754	23971	23971	59746	59746	07985	07985
74026	74206	36981	36981	36978	36978	02547	20547
03697	03697	29478	92478	29087	29087	09804	09804

95876	95867	49876	49876	45984	45684	65987	65987
69569	69569	39857	93857	36952	36952	36542	36542
60945	60945	09587	09587	36978	36978	06589	06589
74598	74598	39496	39496	36540	36540	69896	66896

39878	39878	26487	26487	55597	55579	06955	06955
39854	39584	36985	36985	69856	69856	39878	39878
78952	78952	44958	44958	23147	23147	39547	39547
26870	26870	65885	65855	21352	21352	95252	92525

29546	29546	78594	78594	88759	87759	65985	65985
96856	96856	36654	36645	96658	96658	36547	36547
36475	39475	06659	06659	23265	23265	36202	36200
35985	35985	95368	95368	35574	35574	39854	39854

58946	58646	49545	49545	36985	36985	59778	59718
32998	32998	29542	23542	85454	85554	95135	95135
79564	79564	02695	02695	49524	49524	36495	36495
29854	29854	29647	29647	29548	29548	89651	89651

Sheet 4

489575 489575	748596 478596	587458 587458	458759 458159
659564 659564	365689 365689	698954 698954	369851 369851
239543 239543	194587 194587	365897 365897	355978 355978
239502 239520	957629 957629	293547 263547	298534 298534
589658 589658	259687 259681	293548 293548	857496 857496
265647 266547	367951 367951	985674 985674	664594 664594
095534 095534	236459 236459	951743 957143	598789 598789
298750 298750	779658 779658	397894 397894	898778 897878
559875 559875	557893 557983	447953 447953	559865 556865
366984 366984	006254 006254	395884 395884	325487 325487
594785 954785	065580 065580	294989 294989	698547 698547
200156 200156	100657 100657	239547 239574	399854 399854
557896 557896	005269 005269	598745 598744	226589 226589
699874 999874	298598 298598	698635 698635	998456 998456
369852 369852	559874 559874	364478 364478	366479 633479
194597 194597	259334 529334	915875 915875	915874 915874
587595 857595	115697 115697	475896 475896	479658 479658
152637 152637	369856 369856	157565 157565	698984 698984
369851 369851	136589 136589	569841 569841	265987 265997
036596 036596	369854 366854	005965 055965	395024 395024
524632 524632	574965 574965	447958 447958	498756 498756
369857 369857	366989 366689	336985 336985	369854 369854
103355 013355	498956 498956	259535 259555	159753 519753
005098 005098	069578 069578	159787 159787	007589 007589
852369 852369	498785 498785	447859 447859	159683 159693
888695 888695	298533 298583	369545 369545	359687 359687
996696 996696	698547 698547	369852 369352	169598 169598
669869 699869	059423 059423	065895 065895	598632 598632

Sheet 5

145664 145664	559865 559865
668859 668859	447859 447859
657495 567495	668563 668563
225698 225698	332569 382569

598654 568654	668597 668597
589631 589631	321596 321596
135986 135986	658714 658114
337489 337489	364587 364587

558754 588754	547856 547856
698653 698653	856472 856472
253659 253659	325698 325668
497846 497846	331456 331456

475825 475825	123658 123658
368541 368451	965413 965413
154875 154875	325987 395287
265987 265987	654986 654986

552699 552699	448554 448554
335984 335984	222598 222598
487596 487569	555525 555555
366521 366521	665466 665466

486698 486698	699335 699335
659545 569545	333639 333639
444445 444445	996369 996339
188746 188746	569654 569654

778549 778549	447896 447896
699552 699552	669856 669568
335433 335433	664875 664875
332656 332666	555819 555819

445887 445887	559986 559686
969658 969658	669853 669853
295484 295484	336657 336657
336694 366394	365998 365998

669894 669894	558954 558954
559878 559878	779562 775692
292487 292487	335965 335965
336479 339479	239878 239878

778965 778965	498765 498765
558745 554785	298865 298865
698983 698983	298562 298562
331597 331597	269774 269714

559898 559889	447586 447856
259584 259584	663257 663257
497887 497887	795859 795859
966254 966254	298584 298584

559686 559686	447856 487456
663896 663896	663256 663256
335987 335987	669954 669954
115141 115741	598791 598791

336659 336659	447589 447589
598787 598187	336985 336985
546559 546559	195856 195865
963648 963648	003651 003651

775985 775985	995875 995875
369854 639854	555857 555857
236948 236948	563594 593594
298745 298745	116985 116985

Sheet 6

55986 55686	99658 99658	77485 77485	99685 99685
47989 47989	59788 59788	66958 69958	66547 66547
79859 79859	48515 48515	66935 66935	59865 59865
59878 59878	26897 29987	12358 12358	42164 41164
77859 77859	44785 44785	77498 77498	44989 44989
69895 69895	99658 99658	69983 69983	79865 79865
49874 49874	96631 96631	39965 39665	56123 56123
59835 95835	11305 11503	56989 56989	55535 55525
22235 22235	59365 59365	74985 74685	66958 66958
33358 33358	74989 47989	59955 59955	36995 36995
99969 96969	89632 89632	59878 59878	79465 74965
88878 88878	03619 03619	46132 46132	28944 28944

TEST 7

(Alpha-Numerical Comparison)

(You will be given **150 questions** which should be completed using the time limit of **5 minutes**).

*Look at the four pairs of alpha-numerical digits. Circle or highlight the combination pair that **does not** match.*

Sheet 1

j07r	j07r	mv39	mv93	g39j	g39j	p20s	p20s
l086	i086	ru28	ru28	e2k0	e2k0	w95r	w95r
3e5d	3e5d	otr4	otr4	30ri	30ir	ccv4	cav4
u90f	u90f	03w2	03w2	e22f	e22f	fj3a	fj3a
qp20	pq20	hg94	hg94	34r9	34r9	ioa8	ioa8
cme3	cme3	lldk	lldk	e03i	e03i	yo65	yo65
eo03	eo03	30dp	3odp	f3k0	f3k0	v49f	u49f
r30i	r30i	wp20	wp20	mn03	nn03	g349	g349
fl02	fl02	daj5	daj5	fal4	fal4	3r0f	r30f
m98a	m98a	ro75	ro75	5t60	5t60	d04i	d04i
as0i	as0i	fw94	fw94	09n3	09m3	t3i0	t3i0
gf4i	gf4l	rfe0	rfeo	2rfk	2rfk	mda9	mda9
r39k	r39k	d39j	d39j	e20l	e20l	a76v	a76v
ays4	ays4	34tr	34tr	30ri	30ri	b9f7	b9t7
frw9	frw9	vaj3	vak3	3rfa	3rfa	h4k7	h4k7
4t9j	4l9j	30fm	30fm	fa0a	fe0a	4rj9	4rj9
id87	id87	w93k	w03k	da45	da45	m6v4	m6v4
4afa	4afa	cda9	cda9	p6la	p6la	z9ja	z9ja
dvd9	dud9	034r	034r	rf3m	rf3n	x0kp	x0kp
vas9	vas9	4tg4	4tg4	0dfi	0dfi	3r0i	3r0l
r38y	r38y	3r8h	3r8h	4gf8	4gf8	m9y7	n9y7
4t9i	4j9i	56y0	56y0	da0c	da0c	6f90	6f90
3e8a	3e8a	5tgb	5tbg	cw3o	cu3o	0k7r	0k7r
v3b9	v3b9	g402	g402	sa0k	sa0k	er6f	er6f
mx38	mx38	d3h8	d3h8	k7g4	k7g4	qt56	tq56
3r9j	3r9j	39rj	39rl	3fr0	3fr0	0iky	0iky
o02u	0o2u	30de	30de	t75i	t75l	m98t	m98t
sqy8	sqy8	g30w	g30w	69jh	69jh	u9da	u9da

Look at the four pairs of alpha-numerical digits. Circle or highlight the combination pair that **does not** match.

Sheet 2

t3u9	t3u9	58yh	58yh	w43u	w43u	c3m9	c3m9
ti30	ti30	ki90	ki90	9iy7	9yi7	bcv8	bcv8
dau8	dua8	y78d	u78d	6rda	6rda	3reh	3reh
da9f	da9f	dahj	dahj	0jh5	0jh5	fr39	fr93

hg8s	hg8s	q3j8	q8j8	ef6h	fe6h	ghj8	jgh8
s98y	s89y	34r9	34r9	b98g	b98g	f78y	f78y
6trm	6trm	dd7k	dd7k	u72y	u72y	diy4	diy4
m976	m976	fa8y	fa8y	t7tj	t7tj	r3j8	r3j8

d59m	d59m	vb49	vb49	v4h9	v4h9	h48h	h48h
54y0	54y0	4tg4	4tg4	45r8	45r8	4ty9	4ty6
gh43	gh34	hj60	hl60	76d6	76b6	df74	df74
y409	y409	dn57	dn57	o87g	o87g	4t0m	4t0m

yr3r	yr3r	593i	593i	gt7j	gt7j	4tk7	4tk7
34a0	34a0	3k5b	3k5d	vh34	v3h4	3nh6	3nh6
mn7s	mn7s	g9s6	g9s6	k6l4	k6l4	a89g	a89j
df3g	bf3g	9l6j	9l6j	lia8	lia8	h9bv	h9bv

4t8u	4t8u	ad7f	a7df	j86f	j86f	69if	69if
w30k	w03k	f86m	f86m	5d8l	5d8l	9g4m	9g4m
0l8j	0l8j	g7kl	g7kl	9k7d	9k7d	t38h	t38h
00o8	00o8	7ka8	7ka8	mx38	mx83	d39j	j39d

8yh6	8yh6	56dj	56dj	g40y	g40y	3tr9	3tr9
7g6d	7g6d	9k7d	9k7d	49jf	49jf	f8m6	f3m6
9k7g	9k7g	9rib	9crib	y0ma	y0ma	a6g8	a6g8
6f60	6f90	vma8	vma8	a89t	a98t	lg93	lg93

l085	l085	3ey4	3ye4	c39m	a39m	m6gs	m6gs
f46y	f46y	0mk8	0mk8	4t9j	4t9j	30d8	30d8
2w5j	2w5j	t8j3	t8j3	f3qp	f3qp	8d6j	86dj
6j8l	6l8j	c7n9	c7n9	3r9i	3r9i	0c62	0c62

*Look at the four pairs of alpha-numerical digits. Circle or highlight the combination pair that **does not** match.*

Sheet 3

4gt8h	4gt8h	a5f8m	a5f8m	g4hak	g4hak	2w9m8	2w9m8
t4r35	t4r35	gf94k	gf94k	0ala6	0aal6	93ka7	93ka7
9c4j3	9a4j3	4g9ja	4j9ja	f0m7h	f0m7h	0m37a	0m37a
30d3k	30d3k	40wpd	40wpd	39jfa	39jfa	48r3a	48r3e

t34a4	t34a4	a5c8m	a5c8m	3r7u9	3r7u9	23e6a	23e6a
0my7a	0my7a	49gf6	49gf6	r3ua6	r3ua6	95ma0	95ma0
49tay	94tay	d9ma0	9dma0	0m637	0n637	8yt3a	8yt3a
c78ma	c78ma	s9du3	s9du3	v4na5	v4na5	a8tke	a8kte

vg49m	vg49m	74mj9	74mj9	3r8ja	3r8ja	vg4ma	vg4ma
ad8j7	ad8j7	46dl8	46ld8	s98ya	s98ay	9fha7	9fha7
dmwoa	dmowa	a6m7s	a6m7s	0m6a7	0m6a7	59md7	59nd7
bfe9k	bfe9k	c7sn9	c7sn9	49kas	49kas	a9ja6	a9ja6

t3y9k	t3y9k	hg49m	gh49m	23d6g	23d6g	g48ja	g48ja
lp9a8	lp9a8	34rf9h	34rf9h	9m8g5	9m8g5	34r9k	34r9k
a8n90	a8n09	38rga	38rga	3r7gn	3r7gu	94u5j	94u5j
0aj6f	0aj6f	9k8ya	9k8ya	39fh0	39fh0	45ty9	45yt9

vb47e	vb47e	y48au	y48au	g8ujf	g8ujf	p8yat	p8tay
df93k	df93k	0l8ta	ol8ta	9ky58	9ky58	afsj8	afsj8
0lkq7	0lkq7	9kam4	9kam4	30k7t	30k7t	da85j	da85j
a9uh0	a9hu0	d0k5a	d0k5a	7kv47	7vk47	b9f6a	b9f6a

k908a	k908a	78yt4	78yt4	9iu8t	9iu8t	g49ik	g49ik
00o7a	o0o7a	l7ewa	l7ewa	p09q7	p09q7	c4ja8	c4ja8
a6td9	a6td9	0oam4	o0am4	q8r76	q8r67	qo28a	go28a
bvm8a	bvm8a	t348a	t348a	v8d6a	v8d6a	a9lac	a9lac

0ot48	0ot48	j874a	j874a	23r3k	23r3k	8v7a6	8v7a6
e5mi5	e5mi5	a9kl3	a9k3l	r3mk4	r3km4	a8r6a	a8r6a
594ka	594ak	lel39	lel39	9fm4a	9fm4a	0lo7d	olo7d
9obm5	9obm5	ut47a	ut47a	9ub7a	9ub7a	d7c9n	d7c9n

Look at the four pairs of alpha-numerical digits. Circle or highlight the combination pair that **does not** match.

Sheet 4

94f8h	94f8h	w8fr7	w8fr7	5y0a8	5y0a8	4r7a0	4r7a0
3r7ah	3r7ah	d7yms	d7yms	a8n03	an803	p9m7d	p9m7d
2me38	2em38	8v7b6	8v76b	r49j8	r49j8	s8f9h	s8f9f
e7r9b	e7r9b	n7f5a	n7f5a	0old7	0old7	bn9d7	bn9d7

8u7t6	8u7t6	y74ja	y74ja	q4r7y	q4r7y	s56g8	s56g8
q5f79	q5f79	a8wla	a8lwa	y9n3d	y9n3d	8g7d5	8g7d5
b9ma8	b9ma8	o08ar	o08ar	cv4ma	cv4am	47mf9	47mf9
9uiaj	9iuaj	385n7	385n7	b8amf	b8amf	27d0h	27dho

45t8u	45t8u	p0i98	p0i98	t934m	t934m	5r8u0	5r8u0
a9u7t	a9u7t	u876t	u876t	a8ulf	a8ulf	0l8ut	0l8tu
y76t9	u76t9	6tiqm	6tqim	mc8dg	mc8gd	a7ymi	a7ymi
89v8d	89v8d	m8ak5	m8ak5	c9ja5	c9ja5	7y5re	7y5re

q4r67	q4r67	45eru	45eru	9ikt7	9ikt7	yu59m	yu59m
78u6t	78u6t	9ki7t	9ki7t	3r03o	3r03o	4t9ua	4t9ua
8kk6a	8kk6a	8y6ra	8y6ar	e8sy7	easy7	9k8yg	9k8gy
7ahag	7haag	19mk6	19mk6	t48ua	t48ua	r38nc	r38nc

t48ua	t48ua	h57yq	h57yq	t47yi	t47yi	e239k	e239k
9k4y7	9k4y7	q87ek	q87ek	p0o8u	p0o8u	asy9n	asy9n
we7ya	we7ya	e7rol	e7rol	a7ydn	7aydn	dadhy	daddy
9mk8h	9nk8h	g89j4	g98j4	27ehf	27ehf	sd8uf	sd8uf

23m7d	23m7d	t4yay	t4yay	u8e3i	u8e3i	4t84u	4t84u
jhd3a	jhd3a	qsu82	qsu82	s9ai2	s9ai2	37an5	37an5
939ad	993ad	8de2u	8de2u	29iam	92iam	9b7aj	b97aj
8fr3j	8fr3j	8uj3a	8vj3a	e9am2	e9am2	d8uak	d8uak

il08t	il08t	yr73a	yr73a	t48ua	t48ua	5y95k	5y95k
t4i9e	t4i9e	d23ma	d23ma	23eka	23eka	t934j	t934l
e29ua	e29ua	a8hr3	a8hr8	xs9k3	xs93k	d89wu	d89wu
mf39a	fm39a	e93ja	e93ja	z8ja5	z8ja5	as8u3	as8u3

Look at the four pairs of alpha-numerical digits. Circle or highlight the combination pair that **does not** match.

Sheet 5

47yt48 47yt48	h7k9d5 h7k9d5	i9l0k9 i9l0k9	345tua 345tua
t4uam3 t4uam3	cm39ha cm39ha	d83uai d83uai	349ak9 349ak9
t39iai t39iai	f39ajr f39arj	sd3iap sd3iap	as8u37 as8u37
43aeu3 43eau3	349aj4 349aj4	a9idam a9iadm	fk9a83 kf9a83
yr36u8 yr36u8	59tjma 59tjma	t48amo t48amo	xzu78a xzu78a
t4ju9a t4ju9a	0kl8u8 0kl8u8	lo9jd7 io9jd7	zi9km6 zi9km6
f39mai f39mia	89u7t6 89v7t6	dy8jr3 dy8jr3	sak95a sak95a
bmia94 bmia94	65b8k0 65b8k0	r3k9ar r3k9ar	dkw95o wkd95o
u6y564 u6y564	j84jfh j84jfh	v5j7o8 v5j708	fj4j6o fj4j6o
r03o87 r03o87	h834k3 h834k3	ihy54r ihy54r	o8u646 o8u646
t48umg t48mug	e3iu9a e3iu9a	j6g4ae j6g4ae	c4as78 c4as87
l0f48a l0f48a	u8r3k8 8ur3k8	k75fd5 k75fd5	n6b546 n6b546
y4u8a0 y4u8a0	8v4m83 8v4m83	15rq17 15rg17	45tui4 45tui4
94ri8u 94ri8u	389ruf 389ruf	9ki47d 9ki47d	r45945 r45945
6tr9n3 6tr6n3	g49is4 g49is4	r398ur r398ur	cm8t57 mc8t57
2746n4 2746n4	r49ia7 r94ia7	0lo84j 0lo84j	t4u49r t4u49r
vm48u8 vm48u3	cm388u cm388u	35tru9 35tru9	4598r4 4598r4
r348ur r348ur	598gtk 598gtk	649frk 649frk	978t6e 978t6e
r93ia0 r93ia0	48rk4m 48kr4m	e2u9j3 2eu9j3	867yt9 867ty9
pl4idj pl4idj	09g8m4 09g8m4	6m8d6d 6m8d6d	248a78 248a78
4t87u4 4t87u4	9445r3 9445r3	358fr4 358fr4	34dh3a 34bh3a
49t49i 49t49i	98jr47 98jr47	9573c8 9573c8	39k57a 39k57a
et5i95 et5i95	3748i6 3748i6	87dh76 78dh76	5na7m5 5na7m5
3958r9 3985r9	278eu3 278ue3	098dy8 098dy8	983ma8 983ma8
r39a8a r39a0a	469ut4 469ut4	459dak 459dak	t49iak t49iak
n697a6 n697a6	86j48a 68j48a	r3yu8a r3yu8a	dfk49a dfk49a
96ma95 96ma95	78ash7 78ash7	u48ah2 v48ah2	fm48ua fm48ua
plcv48 plcv48	34e8a3 34e8a3	js82a8 js82a8	458f4m 458f4n

Look at the four pairs of alpha-numerical digits. Circle or highlight the combination pair that does not match.

Sheet 6

4tt47	4tt47	23e8a	23e8a	4t90i	4t90i	457a6	457a6
t69i4	t69i4	49tia	49tia	f48ua	f84ua	94o93	94o93
df9ua	df9va	94y5p	94j5p	648aj	648aj	2n848	2o848
gf49u	gf49u	9isak	9isak	54ma7	54ma7	i4370	i4370

t8u4a	t8v4a	tr4u8	tr48u	k8g4h	k8g4h	349ua	349ua
f49ur	f49ur	werop	werop	f4j8a	f4ja8	37fh4	37hf4
u4u09	u4u09	3539f	3539f	nc38a	nc38a	2b3m6	2b3m6
k89t4	k89t4	j8g4a	j8g4a	9ujd3	9ujd3	3nm8a	3nm8a

8ut4s	3ut4s	i478g	i478g
496f4	496f4	gj348	gj348
9k8ya	9k8ya	ngf84	gnf84
78a9p	78a9p	bh48a	bh48a

ANSWERS TO *TEST 7*

Sheet 1

j07r	j07r	mv39	mv93	g39j	g39j	p20s	p20s
l086	i086	ru28	ru28	e2k0	e2k0	w95r	w95r
3e5d	3e5d	otr4	otr4	30ri	30ir	ccv4	cav4
u90f	u90f	03w2	03w2	e22f	e22f	fj3a	fj3a

qp20	pq20	hg94	hg94	34r9	34r9	ioa8	ioa8
cme3	cme3	lldk	lldk	e03i	e03i	yo65	yo65
eo03	eo03	30dp	3odp	f3k0	f3k0	v49f	u49f
r30i	r30i	wp20	wp20	mn03	nn03	g349	g349

fl02	fl02	daj5	daj5	fal4	fal4	3r0f	r30f
m98a	m98a	ro75	ro75	5t60	5t60	d04i	d04i
as0i	as0i	fw94	fw94	09n3	09m3	t3i0	t3i0
gf4i	gf4l	rfe0	rfeo	2rfk	2rfk	mda9	mda9

r39k	r39k	d39j	d39j	e20l	e20l	a76v	a76v
ays4	ays4	34tr	34tr	30ri	30ri	b9f7	b9t7
frw9	frw9	vaj3	vak3	3rfa	3rfa	h4k7	h4k7
4t9j	4l9j	30fm	30fm	fa0a	fe0a	4rj9	4rj9

id87	id87	w93k	w03k	da45	da45	m6v4	m6v4
4afa	4afa	cda9	cda9	p6la	p6la	z9ja	z9ja
dvd9	dud9	034r	034r	rf3m	rf3n	x0kp	x0kp
vas9	vas9	4tg4	4tg4	0dfi	0dfi	3r0i	3r0l

r38y	r38y	3r8h	3r8h	4gf8	4gf8	m9y7	n9y7
4t9i	4j9i	56y0	56y0	da0c	da0c	6f90	6f90
3e8a	3e8a	5tgb	5tbg	cw3o	cu3o	0k7r	0k7r
v3b9	v3b9	g402	g402	sa0k	sa0k	er6f	er6f

mx38	mx38	d3h8	d3h8	k7g4	k7g4	qt56	tq56
3r9j	3r9j	39rj	39rl	3fr0	3fr0	0iky	0iky
o02u	0o2u	30de	30de	t75i	t75l	m98t	m98t
sqy8	sqy8	g30w	g30w	69jh	69jh	u9da	u9da

Sheet 2

t3u9　t3u9 ti30　ti30 dau8　dua8 da9f　da9f	58yh　58yh ki90　ki90 y78d　u78d dahj　dahj	w43u　w43u 9iy7　9yi7 6rda　6rda 0jh5　0jh5	c3m9　c3m9 bcv8　bcv8 3reh　3reh fr39　fr93
hg8s　hg8s s98y　s89y 6trm　6trm m976　m976	q3j8　q8j8 34r9　34r9 dd7k　dd7k fa8y　fa8y	ef6h　fe6h b98g　b98g u72y　u72y t7tj　t7tj	ghj8　jgh8 f78y　f78y diy4　diy4 r3j8　r3j8
d59m　d59m 54y0　54y0 gh43　gh34 y409　y409	vb49　vb49 4tg4　4tg4 hj60　hl60 dn57　dn57	v4h9　v4h9 45r8　45r8 76d6　76b6 o87g　o87g	h48h　h48h 4ty9　4ty6 df74　df74 4t0m　4t0m
yr3r　yr3r 34a0　34a0 mn7s　mn7s df3g　bf3g	593i　593i 3k5b　3k5d g9s6　g9s6 9l6j　9l6j	gt7j　gt7j vh34　v3h4 k6l4　k6l4 lia8　lia8	4tk7　4tk7 3nh6　3nh6 a89g　a89j h9bv　h9bv
4t8u　4t8u w30k　w03k 0l8j　0l8j 00o8　00o8	ad7f　a7df f86m　f86m g7kl　g7kl 7ka8　7ka8	j86f　j86f 5d8l　5d8l 9k7d　9k7d mx38　mx83	69if　69if 9g4m　9g4m t38h　t38h d39j　j39d
8yh6　8yh6 7g6d　7g6d 9k7g　9k7g 6f60　6f90	56dj　56dj 9k7d　9k7d 9rib　9crib vma8　vma8	g40y　g40y 49jf　49jf y0ma　y0ma a89t　a98t	3tr9　3tr9 f8m6　f3m6 a6g8　a6g8 lg93　lg93
l085　l085 f46y　f46y 2w5j　2w5j 6j8l　6l8j	3ey4　3ye4 0mk8　0mk8 t8j3　t8j3 c7n9　c7n9	c39m　a39m 4t9j　4t9j f3qp　f3qp 3r9i　3r9i	m6gs　m6gs 30d8　30d8 8d6j　86dj 0c62　0c62

Sheet 3

4gt8h	4gt8h	a5f8m	a5f8m	g4hak	g4hak	2w9m8	2w9m8
t4r35	t4r35	gf94k	gf94k	0ala6	0aal6	93ka7	93ka7
9c4j3	9a4j3	4g9ja	4j9ja	f0m7h	f0m7h	0m37a	0m37a
30d3k	30d3k	40wpd	40wpd	39jfa	39jfa	48r3a	48r3e

t34a4	t34a4	a5c8m	a5c8m	3r7u9	3r7u9	23e6a	23e6a
0my7a	0my7a	49gf6	49gf6	r3ua6	r3ua6	95ma0	95ma0
49tay	94tay	d9ma0	9dma0	0m637	0n637	8yt3a	8yt3a
c78ma	c78ma	s9du3	s9du3	v4na5	v4na5	a8tke	a8kte

vg49m	vg49m	74mj9	74mj9	3r8ja	3r8ja	vg4ma	vg4ma
ad8j7	ad8j7	46dl8	46ld8	s98ya	s98ay	9fha7	9fha7
dmwoa	dmowa	a6m7s	a6m7s	0m6a7	0m6a7	59md7	59nd7
bfe9k	bfe9k	c7sn9	c7sn9	49kas	49kas	a9ja6	a9ja6

t3y9k	t3y9k	hg49m	gh49m	23d6g	23d6g	g48ja	g48ja
lp9a8	lp9a8	34rf9h	34rf9h	9m8g5	9m8g5	34r9k	34r9k
a8n90	a8n09	38rga	38rga	3r7gn	3r7gu	94u5j	94u5j
0aj6f	0aj6f	9k8ya	9k8ya	39fh0	39fh0	45ty9	45yt9

vb47e	vb47e	y48au	y48au	g8ujf	g8ujf	p8yat	p8tay
df93k	df93k	0l8ta	ol8ta	9ky58	9ky58	afsj8	afsj8
0lkq7	0lkq7	9kam4	9kam4	30k7t	30k7t	da85j	da85j
a9uh0	a9hu0	d0k5a	d0k5a	7kv47	7vk47	b9f6a	b9f6a

k908a	k908a	78yt4	78yt4	9iu8t	9iu8t	g49ik	g49ik
00o7a	o0o7a	l7ewa	l7ewa	p09q7	p09q7	c4ja8	c4ja8
a6td9	a6td9	0oam4	o0am4	q8r76	q8r67	qo28a	go28a
bvm8a	bvm8a	t348a	t348a	v8d6a	v8d6a	a9lac	a9lac

0ot48	0ot48	j874a	j874a	23r3k	23r3k	8v7a6	8v7a6
e5mi5	e5mi5	a9kl3	a9k3l	r3mk4	r3km4	a8r6a	a8r6a
594ka	594ak	lel39	lel39	9fm4a	9fm4a	0lo7d	olo7d
9obm5	9obm5	ut47a	ut47a	9ub7a	9ub7a	d7c9n	d7c9n

Sheet 4

94f8h 94f8h 3r7ah 3r7ah 2me38 2em38 e7r9b e7r9b	w8fr7 w8fr7 d7yms d7yms 8v7b6 8v76b n7f5a n7f5a	5y0a8 5y0a8 a8n03 an803 r49j8 r49j8 0old7 0old7	4r7a0 4r7a0 p9m7d p9m7d s8f9h s8f9f bn9d7 bn9d7
8u7t6 8u7t6 q5f79 q5f79 b9ma8 b9ma8 9uiaj 9iuaj	y74ja y74ja a8wla a8lwa o08ar o08ar 385n7 385n7	q4r7y q4r7y y9n3d y9n3d cv4ma cv4am b8amf b8amf	s56g8 s56g8 8g7d5 8g7d5 47mf9 47mf9 27d0h 27dho
45t8u 45t8u a9u7t a9u7t y76t9 u76t9 89v8d 89v8d	p0i98 p0i98 u876t u876t 6tiqm 6tqim m8ak5 m8ak5	t934m t934m a8ulf a8ulf mc8dg mc8gd c9ja5 c9ja5	5r8u0 5r8u0 0l8ut 0l8tu a7ymi a7ymi 7y5re 7y5re
q4r67 q4r67 78u6t 78u6t 8kk6a 8kk6a 7ahag 7haag	45eru 45eru 9ki7t 9ki7t 8y6ra 8y6ar 19mk6 19mk6	9ikt7 9ikt7 3r03o 3r03o e8sy7 easy7 t48ua t48ua	yu59m yu59m 4t9ua 4t9ua 9k8yg 9k8gy r38nc r38nc
t48ua t48ua 9k4y7 9k4y7 we7ya we7ya 9mk8h 9nk8h	h57yq h57yq q87ek q87ek e7rol e7rol g89j4 g98j4	t47yi t47yi p0o8u p0o8u a7ydn 7aydn 27ehf 27ehf	e239k e239k asy9n asy9n dadhy daddy sd8uf sd8uf
23m7d 23m7d jhd3a jhd3a 939ad 993ad 8fr3j 8fr3j	t4yay t4yay qsu82 qsu82 8de2u 8de2u 8uj3a 8vj3a	u8e3i u8e3i s9ai2 s9ai2 29iam 92iam e9am2 e9am2	4t84u 4t84u 37an5 37an5 9b7aj b97aj d8uak d8uak
il08t il08t t4i9e t4i9e e29ua e29ua mf39a fm39a	yr73a yr73a d23ma d23ma a8hr3 a8hr8 e93ja e93ja	t48ua t48ua 23eka 23eka xs9k3 xs93k z8ja5 z8ja5	5y95k 5y95k t934j t934l d89wu d89wu as8u3 as8u3

Sheet 5

47yt48	47yt48	h7k9d5	h7k9d5	i9l0k9	i9l0k9	345tua	345tua
t4uam3	t4uam3	cm39ha	cm39ha	d83uai	d83uai	349ak9	349ak9
t39iai	t39iai	f39ajr	f39arj	sd3iap	sd3iap	as8u37	as8u37
43aeu3	43eau3	349aj4	349aj4	a9idam	a9iadm	fk9a83	kf9a83

yr36u8	yr36u8	59tjma	59tjma	t48amo	t48amo	xzu78a	xzu78a
t4ju9a	t4ju9a	0kl8u8	0kl8u8	lo9jd7	io9jd7	zi9km6	zi9km6
f39mai	f39mia	89u7t6	89v7t6	dy8jr3	dy8jr3	sak95a	sak95a
bmia94	bmia94	65b8k0	65b8k0	r3k9ar	r3k9ar	dkw95o	wkd95o

u6y564	u6y564	j84jfh	j84jfh	v5j7o8	v5j708	fj4j6o	fj4j6o
r03o87	r03o87	h834k3	h834k3	ihy54r	ihy54r	o8u646	o8u646
t48umg	t48mug	e3iu9a	e3iu9a	j6g4ae	j6g4ae	c4as78	c4as87
l0f48a	l0f48a	u8r3k8	8ur3k8	k75fd5	k75fd5	n6b546	n6b546

y4u8a0	y4u8a0	8v4m83	8v4m83	15rq17	15rg17	45tui4	45tui4
94ri8u	94ri8u	389ruf	389ruf	9ki47d	9ki47d	r45945	r45945
6tr9n3	6tr6n3	g49is4	g49is4	r398ur	r398ur	cm8t57	mc8t57
2746n4	2746n4	r49ia7	r94ia7	0lo84j	0lo84j	t4u49r	t4u49r

vm48u8	vm48u3	cm388u	cm388u	35tru9	35tru9	4598r4	4598r4
r348ur	r348ur	598gtk	598gtk	649frk	649frk	978t6e	978t6e
r93ia0	r93ia0	48rk4m	48kr4m	e2u9j3	2eu9j3	867yt9	867ty9
pl4idj	pl4idj	09g8m4	09g8m4	6m8d6d	6m8d6d	248a78	248a78

4t87u4	4t87u4	9445r3	9445r3	358fr4	358fr4	34dh3a	34bh3a
49t49i	49t49i	98jr47	98jr47	9573c8	9573c8	39k57a	39k57a
et5i95	et5i95	3748i6	3748i6	87dh76	78dh76	5na7m5	5na7m5
3958r9	3985r9	278eu3	278ue3	098dy8	098dy8	983ma8	983ma8

r39a8a	r39a0a	469ut4	469ut4	459dak	459dak	t49iak	t49iak
n697a6	n697a6	86j48a	68j48a	r3yu8a	r3yu8a	dfk49a	dfk49a
96ma95	96ma95	78ash7	78ash7	u48ah2	v48ah2	fm48ua	fm48ua
plcv48	plcv48	34e8a3	34e8a3	js82a8	js82a8	458f4m	458f4n

Sheet 6

4tt47	4tt47	23e8a	23e8a	4t90i	4t90i	457a6	457a6
t69i4	t69i4	49tia	49tia	f48ua	f84ua	94o93	94o93
df9ua	df9va	94y5p	94j5p	648aj	648aj	2n848	2o848
gf49u	gf49u	9isak	9isak	54ma7	54ma7	i4370	i4370
t8u4a	t8v4a	tr4u8	tr48u	k8g4h	k8g4h	349ua	349ua
f49ur	f49ur	werop	werop	f4j8a	f4ja8	37fh4	37hf4
u4u09	u4u09	3539f	3539f	nc38a	nc38a	2b3m6	2b3m6
k89t4	k89t4	j8g4a	j8g4a	9ujd3	9ujd3	3nm8a	3nm8a
8ut4s	3ut4s	i478g	i478g				
496f4	496f4	gj348	gj348				
9k8ya	9k8ya	ngf84	gnf84				
78a9p	78a9p	bh48a	bh48a				

TEST 8

(Alpha-Numerical Comparison)

(You will be given **150 questions** which should be completed using the time limit of **5 minutes**).

Look at the four pairs of alpha-numerical digits. Circle or highlight the combination pair that **does not** match.

Sheet 1

58j5	58j5	2b68	2b68	a6tr	a6tr	7y98	7y98
39k3	39k3	m389	m398	0g48	0g48	97h8	97h8
38v2	38u2	938v	938v	3f80	3f80	57n7	57u7
28d9	28d9	384g	384g	98b9	89b9	r879	r879

48a9	48a9	938a	938a	34a7	34a7	20r7	20r7
93g7	937g	3i48	3i48	j645	j645	45l8	45i8
e876	e876	6ma7	6na7	30h1	30h7	5j85	5j85
g986	g986	87p0	87p0	87z7	87z7	53v7	53v7

290a	290a	e335	e335	t439	t439	85j5	85j5
k298	k298	f493	f439	83e8	83e8	36v4	36v4
8r87	8r78	978c	978c	94x6	49x6	694f	649f
08u4	08u4	89g3	89g3	6595	6595	49t8	49t8

495i	495i	q284	q284	48u5	48u5	0o6	0o6
n438	n438	38r9	38r9	b378	b378	58u3	583u
48t7	48t7	49t0	49to	37f4	374f	8h28	8h28
4j31	4l31	23h4	23h4	2y48	2y48	49t5	49t5

4w72	4w72	458f	458f	29t8	29t8	353m	353m
289a	289a	48u4	48v4	48n3	48n3	39c5	39c5
8v03	8vo3	37c3	37c3	39c6	93c6	y739	y793
93m7	93m7	01n5	01n5	30g7	30g7	r842	r842

48j5	48j5	59k5	59k5	37h4	37h4	458m	458m
48d3	48d3	t535	t535	49g3	49g3	45u4	45u4
238d	238d	427f	427j	48j5	48l5	r337	r733
30f4	3of4	7h65	7h65	59h8	59h8	83d8	83d8

8f76	8f76	8f54	f854	48j4	48j4	8475	8475
34d5	34d5	y875	y875	384u	348u	3492	3492
80m7	80n7	o084	o084	3e43	3e43	5374	5347
87h8	87h8	986h	986h	8425	8425	2456	2456

*Look at the four pairs of alpha-numerical digits. Circle or highlight the combination pair that **does not** match.*

Sheet 2

t49u	t49u	450i	450i	2eia	2eia	3r9u	3r9u
f4kr	f4kr	r3u8	r3u8	tu49	tu49	fu4a	fu4a
e39i	e93i	3r9u	3r9u	vm48	mv48	49uf	49fu
adf4	adf4	d39u	d39v	adfp	adfp	596y	596y

4t8u	4t8u	3r8y	3r8y	35r6	35r6	r90i	r9oi
f8ua	f8au	f48a	f48a	g48u	g48u	df48	df48
4t9u	4t9u	48ty	48yt	xc3h	cx3h	pi6a	pi6a
0i47	0i47	4t8a	4t8a	zm84	zm84	450t	450t

t48u	t48u	489g	489g	598g	598g	95y7	95y7
vm50	vm50	v4ad	v4ad	7t7a	7t7a	cb47	cb47
lgu8	igu8	8fya	8fay	a866	a866	axt7	axt7
a8dy	a8dy	ad8y	ad8y	vm48	mv48	xh77	xh17

jg84	jg84	xc46	xc46	kd8a	kd8a	4m6k	4m6k
afj8	afj8	nc48	nc48	8s7g	8s7g	6m8c	6m8c
l9fa	l9af	48gt	84gt	834n	384n	xy73	xy73
v4b8	v4b8	afd8	afd8	a7b3	a7b3	f8o8	fo88

v48h	v48h	4m47	4m47	9u4t	9u4t	4t89	4t89
4tj8	4ti8	v83n	v83n	t49u	t49u	g49j	g49j
f38a	f38a	d83n	d83m	a7y3	a73y	3m8f	m38f
cadf	cadf	gl58	gl58	9p6k	9p6k	cf3m	cf3m

9m6j	9m6j	4t8u	4t8u	4m7o	4m70	f48j	f48l
3m40	3m40	34rk	34rk	sa8m	sa8m	l94j	l94j
kgf89	kgf98	d3j8	d38j	m6na	m6na	4k6h	4k6h
3n5k	3n5k	a8s2	a8s2	49h5	49h5	8nh2	8nh2

5y9u	5y9u	4t9g	4t9g	3i6l	3l6l	g49i	g49i
3l5n	3l5n	h8n3	h3n3	2hy6	2hy6	3mf8	3mf8
6m7l	6n7l	d83k	d83k	x78b	x78b	5mc7	5cm7
3jfv	3jfv	j6l7	j6l7	7h4f	7h4f	eks8	eks8

*Look at the four pairs of alpha-numerical digits. Circle or highlight the combination pair that **does not** match.*

Sheet 3

8gt4y	8gt4y	1m37c	1n37c	53m5j	53m5j	f39k3	f39k3
9jdf3	9jdf3	vc8j4	vc8j4	49g73	49g73	3d39a	3d93a
tki41	tki41	c8g76	c8g76	378f6	378f6	c38a6	c38a6
4j84l	4l84l	3jd75	3jd75	3nc64	3cn64	x82no	x82no
l29d8	l29d8	38ru3	38ru3	4r8u2	4r8u2	g489u	g489v
as7y8	as7y8	49u8d	49u8d	3r9is	3r9is	f37y3	f37y3
7yh3m	7hy3m	d38y8	d3y88	d238	d238	g487y	g487y
6j9f4	6j9f4	39il9	39il9	aut2e	aute2	d376t	d376t
48u3o	48u3o	48g8a	48g8a	b48ud	b48ud	f39ui	f39ui
d38ua	d38ua	d3at6	d3at6	g37ya	g3y7a	cj348	cj384
s27yf	s27yf	3ipx7	3lpx7	cen85	cen85	xa95f	xa95f
49tm4	94tm4	g4ma7	g4ma7	v5mx7	v5mx7	59tui	59tui
i483a	l483a	g49ju	g49ju	4tu9a	4tu9a	ju84j	jv84j
t38u8	t38u8	lkad8	lkad8	39aj3	39aj3	ah874	ah874
ahjc3	ahjc3	alsff	alstf	cn38a	nc38a	s28sd	s28sd
5m9sa	5m9sa	tu48a	tu48a	a0so2	a0so2	ce4j8	ce4j8
g49dk	g49dk	c3ud3	c3ud3	b4j8u	b4j8u	g49iy	g49iy
d3k9a	d3k9a	d3jad	d3jad	498f4	49f84	t48ud	t48ud
u45k9	u54k9	l398u	l398v	98e28	98e28	d3y7t	d3u7t
g4y8a	g4y8a	r39ud	r39ud	37n83	37n83	48udl	48udl
h58um	h58um	4ty94	4ty94	84tu4	84tu4	59ti7	59ti7
5t8ur	58tur	934uj	934uj	47hg5	47hg5	3e6t5	3e6t5
t7yo5	t7yo5	e27t3	e27t3	9i6y4	9l6y4	9ig45	9gi45
549it	549it	796u6	976u6	12t3u	12t3u	3v7t4	3v7t4
5y89u	5u89u	ui83j	ui83j	t348j	t348i	4tu8j	4tu8j
gt45h	gt45h	cbn65	cbn65	sd3n8	sd3n8	f37g3	f37g3
f4h7m	f4h7m	rj39a	ri39a	c48jr	c48jr	83ur6	83ur6
698u8	698u8	cm9a8	cm9a8	85rjm	85rjm	498tw	49t8w

Look at the four pairs of alpha-numerical digits. Circle or highlight the combination pair that **does not** match.

Sheet 4

5t8u5	5t8u5	4gt8y	4gt8y	6t8u9	6t8u9	3e9im	3e9im
ru489	ru489	c4n7g	c47ng	o67r4	067r4	3g403	3g403
b5t53	bt553	d37g2	d37g2	65r78	65r78	4g4ju	4g4jv
lr93u	lr93u	ei39j	ei39j	78y5i	78y5i	j9f8g	j9f8g

4gt94	4gt94	49ud3	49ud3	v48hy	v48hu	48u36	48u36
c3j9u	c3j9u	d90i5	d90i5	y5j8s	y5j8s	59i6y	59i6y
87yd3	87ud3	g437t	y437t	45t8u	45t8u	ry84d	ry34d
d39ao	d39ao	48ru3	48ru3	9if3h	9if3h	48t5k	48t5k

590u4	59u04	4t8u3	4t8u3	34ru3	34ru3	4tr8u	4tr8u
ef3y7	ef3y7	d38ha	d3h8a	5yi57	5yi57	f48ud	f48ud
d3nh8	d3nh8	489u7	489u7	48b53	48d53	0fi9o	0fi9o
96j37	96j37	rj892	rj892	548hj	548hj	4t94u	49t4u

76ty8	76ty8	4tr8u	4tr8u	gf478	gf478	g48j0	g48j0
56r6t	56r6t	4609j	46o9j	4tru4	4tru4	409tu	409tu
7j98r	7i98r	48n63	48n63	9ity3	city3	9uy64	9vy64
x58e4	x58e4	34f94	34f94	93i57	93i57	47y3h	47y3h

4t8u4	4t8u4	48tu4	48tu4	4fu89	4fu89	4t9i4	4t9i4
y49id	y49id	39i63	39i63	909h3	906h3	347h4	347h4
4t9iw	4t9iw	um382	um238	29dj2	29dj2	0k783	ok783
39ri3	36ri3	r39ui	r39ui	0emj3	0emj3	384h6	384h6

49tu4	49tu4	f48uf	f48uf	209ru	209ru	48t4j	48t4j
256ek	256ek	489u3	489u3	9f3j7	9f3j7	f4j9a	f4j9a
906i5	609i5	398u4	938u4	j8grh	j8grh	9k3h5	9k3h5
8nt84	8nt84	6ru3j	6ru3j	fjr9f	fjrf9	40kf8	40fk8

iu4yu	iu4yu	4t8u4	4t8u4	u8er3	u8er3	4t8u4	4t8u4
f48hd	t48hd	90iy6	90iy6	as8u1	as8u1	90i73	90l73
902me	902me	6j87h	6j87h	k945j	k945j	49tui	49tui
908uy	908uy	g7hi8	g7h8i	049itr	049tir	9i5kg	9i5kg

*Look at the four pairs of alpha-numerical digits. Circle or highlight the combination pair that **does not** match.*

Sheet 5

489ur4	489ru4	h9d39k	h9d39k	3er3uo	3eu3ro	t4j943	t4t943
73yre3	73yre3	mk9hd2	mk9dh2	dk392a	dk392a	39ri3h	39ri3h
09i5t5	09i5t5	ns2m1k	ns2m1k	9ih58f	9ih58f	d29jd0	d29jd0
4r9i32	4r9i32	je29h3	je29h3	rjk90r	rjk90r	9ui7yf	9ui7yf
9056k5	9056k5	58tu5j	58tu5j	45rf7y	54rf7y	4tioj4	4tioj4
384jr4	384jr4	t5j89t	f5j89t	98u76p	98u76p	26we20	26we20
37ye35	73ye35	9ik98u	9ik98u	87y45e	87y45e	r38u35	r83u35
94i54h	94i54h	j89jto	j89jto	h785r5	h785r5	d38ua3	d38ua3
5t8u53	5t8u53	4t94ia	4t94ia	4t84ua	4t84ua	tg489u	gt489u
e392sm	e392sm	38uf34	38uf34	398urk	398urk	h4978g	h4978g
0i48u4	0i48u4	90i3ka	9oi3ka	90i7yd	90l7yd	98yu4d	98yu4d
8u5n46	8v5n46	389uar	389uar	8uas2a	8uas2a	387ry3	387ry3
t58uf4	t58uf4	4t49ia	4t49ia	98u73h	98u37h	4t894u	4t894u
u90ir3	u90ir3	983yr3	938yr3	y767h3	y767h3	gf378y	gf378y
36tr3t	36fr3t	430ui4	430ui4	ui897n	ui897n	598ug5	598gu5
590i54	590i54	89u394	89u394	e3j82a	e3j82a	u578y5	u578y5
589ugt5	589ugt5	67h8g4	67h8g4	ei3984	ei3984	4t49if	4t49if
t498ut	t498ut	98u3j3	98u3j3	it949u	it499u	lly585	lly585
98uij4	98uij4	09i3j2	09l3j2	t84u8a	t84u8a	489irl	49i8rl
98u3e3	98v3e3	08u2e3	08u2e3	r389uf	r389uf	jr47lo	jr47lo
4t9u4k	4t9u4k	4t490if	4t490if	hg834j	hg834j	op5tiu	op5tiu
9fi34a	9fi34a	102ok3	102ok3	f4j9al	f4j9al	ti59um	ti59um
j9s2lk	j9s2lk	1946mj	1964mj	jd29aj	dj29aj	r4u8ny	r4u8ny
bnb832	bbn832	6k954r	6k954r	j93jad	j93jad	y9imy5	y6imy5
329jkf	329jkf	537974	537974	vxcmbf	vxcmbf	249uir	49uir
90if3j	9oif3j	453972	453792	teyuiq	teyuiq	da8d3k	da8d3k
907533	907533	529756	529756	pkldwh	pkldwh	9i3rnj	9i3nrj
etueom	etueom	537982	537982	opurjt	opvrjt	8j4nj5	8j4nj5

*Look at the four pairs of alpha-numerical digits. Circle or highlight the combination pair that **does not** match.*

Sheet 6

7y9i	7y9i	r37y	r37y	538u	538u	58m3	58m3
7ty76	7ty76	fj38	fj38	e38f	e38f	58c8	58c8
64er	64re	gn48	gn48	64j6	64j6	37yd	73yd
k90i	k90i	hri3	hir3	c7bv	c7vb	d76t	d76t

38uj	38uj	53uf	53uf	5378	5738	4t49	4t49
nso9	sno9	tj49	tj49	po38	po38	fr3j	fr3j
bb49	bb49	as87	as87	ju85	ju85	d3h7	d3h7
p93u	p93u	ite4	lte4	f74j	f74j	89j4	98j4

r38u	r38u	fe38	fe38
4r8u	4r8u	a389	a389
c4m9	cm49	d38f	d38f
lt49	lt49	p39p	p30p

ANSWERS TO *TEST 8*

Sheet 1

58j5	58j5	2b68	2b68	a6tr	a6tr	7y98	7y98
39k3	39k3	m389	m398	0g48	0g48	97h8	97h8
38v2	38u2	938v	938v	3f80	3f80	57n7	57u7
28d9	28d9	384g	384g	98b9	89b9	r879	r879

48a9	48a9	938a	938a	34a7	34a7	20r7	20r7
93g7	937g	3i48	3i48	j645	j645	45l8	45i8
e876	e876	6ma7	6na7	30h1	30h7	5j85	5j85
g986	g986	87p0	87p0	87z7	87z7	53v7	53v7

290a	290a	e335	e335	t439	t439	85j5	85j5
k298	k298	f493	f439	83e8	83e8	36v4	36v4
8r87	8r78	978c	978c	94x6	49x6	694f	649f
08u4	08u4	89g3	89g3	6595	6595	49t8	49t8

495i	495i	q284	q284	48u5	48u5	0o6	0o6
n438	n438	38r9	38r9	b378	b378	58u3	583u
48t7	48t7	49t0	49to	37f4	374f	8h28	8h28
4j31	4l31	23h4	23h4	2y48	2y48	49t5	49t5

4w72	4w72	458f	458f	29t8	29t8	353m	353m
289a	289a	48u4	48v4	48n3	48n3	39c5	39c5
8v03	8vo3	37c3	37c3	39c6	93c6	y739	y793
93m7	93m7	01n5	01n5	30g7	30g7	r842	r842

48j5	48j5	59k5	59k5	37h4	37h4	458m	458m
48d3	48d3	t535	t535	49g3	49g3	45u4	45u4
238d	238d	427f	427j	48j5	48l5	r337	r733
30f4	3of4	7h65	7h65	59h8	59h8	83d8	83d8

8f76	8f76	8f54	f854	48j4	48j4	8475	8475
34d5	34d5	y875	y875	384u	348u	3492	3492
80m7	80n7	o084	o084	3e43	3e43	5374	5347
87h8	87h8	986h	986h	8425	8425	2456	2456

Sheet 2

t49u t49u	450i 450i	2eia 2eia	3r9u 3r9u
f4kr f4kr	r3u8 r3u8	tu49 tu49	fu4a fu4a
e39i e93i	3r9u 3r9u	vm48 mv48	49uf 49fu
adf4 adf4	d39u d39v	adfp adfp	596y 596y

4t8u 4t8u	3r8y 3r8y	35r6 35r6	r90i r9oi
f8ua f8au	f48a f48a	g48u g48u	df48 df48
4t9u 4t9u	48ty 48yt	xc3h cx3h	pi6a pi6a
0i47 0i47	4t8a 4t8a	zm84 zm84	450t 450t

t48u t48u	489g 489g	598g 598g	95y7 95y7
vm50 vm50	v4ad v4ad	7t7a 7t7a	cb47 cb47
lgu8 igu8	8fya 8fay	a866 a866	axt7 axt7
a8dy a8dy	ad8y ad8y	vm48 mv48	xh77 xh17

jg84 jg84	xc46 xc46	kd8a kd8a	4m6k 4m6k
afj8 afj8	nc48 nc48	8s7g 8s7g	6m8c 6m8c
l9fa l9af	48gt 84gt	834n 384n	xy73 xy73
v4b8 v4b8	afd8 afd8	a7b3 a7b3	f8o8 fo88

v48h v48h	4m47 4m47	9u4t 9u4t	4t89 4t89
4tj8 4ti8	v83n v83n	t49u t49u	g49j g49j
f38a f38a	d83n d83m	a7y3 a73y	3m8f m38f
cadf cadf	gl58 gl58	9p6k 9p6k	cf3m cf3m

9m6j 9m6j	4t8u 4t8u	4m7o 4m70	f48j f48l
3m40 3m40	34rk 34rk	sa8m sa8m	l94j l94j
kgf89 kgf98	d3j8 d38j	m6na m6na	4k6h 4k6h
3n5k 3n5k	a8s2 a8s2	49h5 49h5	8nh2 8nh2

5y9u 5y9u	4t9g 4t9g	3i6l 3l6l	g49i g49i
3l5n 3l5n	h8n3 h3n3	2hy6 2hy6	3mf8 3mf8
6m7l 6n7l	d83k d83k	x78b x78b	5mc7 5cm7
3jfv 3jfv	j6l7 j6l7	7h4f 7h4f	eks8 eks8

Sheet 3

8gt4y 8gt4y	1m37c 1n37c	53m5j 53m5j	f39k3 f39k3
9jdf3 9jdf3	vc8j4 vc8j4	49g73 49g73	3d39a 3d93a
tki41 tki41	c8g76 c8g76	378f6 378f6	c38a6 c38a6
4j84l 4l84l	3jd75 3jd75	3nc64 3cn64	x82no x82no
l29d8 l29d8	38ru3 38ru3	4r8u2 4r8u2	g489u g489v
as7y8 as7y8	49u8d 49u8d	3r9is 3r9is	f37y3 f37y3
7yh3m 7hy3m	d38y8 d3y88	d238 d238	g487y g487y
6j9f4 6j9f4	39il9 39il9	aut2e aute2	d376t d376t
48u3o 48u3o	48g8a 48g8a	b48ud b48ud	f39ui f39ui
d38ua d38ua	d3at6 d3at6	g37ya g3y7a	cj348 cj384
s27yf s27yf	3ipx7 3lpx7	cen85 cen85	xa95f xa95f
49tm4 94tm4	g4ma7 g4ma7	v5mx7 v5mx7	59tui 59tui
i483a l483a	g49ju g49ju	4tu9a 4tu9a	ju84j jv84j
t38u8 t38u8	lkad8 lkad8	39aj3 39aj3	ah874 ah874
ahjc3 ahjc3	alsff alstf	cn38a nc38a	s28sd s28sd
5m9sa 5m9sa	tu48a tu48a	a0so2 a0so2	ce4j8 ce4j8
g49dk g49dk	c3ud3 c3ud3	b4j8u b4j8u	g49iy g49iy
d3k9a d3k9a	d3jad d3jad	498f4 49f84	t48ud t48ud
u45k9 u54k9	l398u l398v	98e28 98e28	d3y7t d3u7t
g4y8a g4y8a	r39ud r39ud	37n83 37n83	48udl 48udl
h58um h58um	4ty94 4ty94	84tu4 84tu4	59ti7 59ti7
5t8ur 58tur	934uj 934uj	47hg5 47hg5	3e6t5 3e6t5
t7yo5 t7yo5	e27t3 e27t3	9i6y4 9l6y4	9ig45 9gi45
549it 549it	796u6 976u6	12t3u 12t3u	3v7t4 3v7t4
5y89u 5u89u	ui83j ui83j	t348j t348i	4tu8j 4tu8j
gt45h gt45h	cbn65 cbn65	sd3n8 sd3n8	f37g3 f37g3
f4h7m f4h7m	rj39a ri39a	c48jr c48jr	83ur6 83ur6
698u8 698u8	cm9a8 cm9a8	85rjm 85rjm	498tw 49t8w

Sheet 4

5t8u5 5t8u5 ru489 ru489 b5t53 bt553 lr93u lr93u	4gt8y 4gt8y c4n7g c47ng d37g2 d37g2 ei39j ei39j	6t8u9 6t8u9 o67r4 067r4 65r78 65r78 78y5i 78y5i	3e9im 3e9im 3g403 3g403 4g4ju 4g4jv j9f8g j9f8g
4gt94 4gt94 c3j9u c3j9u 87yd3 87ud3 d39ao d39ao	49ud3 49ud3 d90i5 d90i5 g437t y437t 48ru3 48ru3	v48hy v48hu y5j8s y5j8s 45t8u 45t8u 9if3h 9if3h	48u36 48u36 59i6y 59i6y ry84d ry34d 48t5k 48t5k
590u4 59u04 ef3y7 ef3y7 d3nh8 d3nh8 96j37 96j37	4t8u3 4t8u3 d38ha d3h8a 489u7 489u7 rj892 rj892	34ru3 34ru3 5yi57 5yi57 48b53 48d53 548hj 548hj	4tr8u 4tr8u f48ud f48ud 0fi9o 0fi9o 4t94u 49t4u
76ty8 76ty8 56r6t 56r6t 7j98r 7i98r x58e4 x58e4	4tr8u 4tr8u 4609j 46o9j 48n63 48n63 34f94 34f94	gf478 gf478 4tru4 4tru4 9ity3 city3 93i57 93i57	g48j0 g48j0 409tu 409tu 9uy64 9vy64 47y3h 47y3h
4t8u4 4t8u4 y49id y49id 4t9iw 4t9iw 39ri3 36ri3	48tu4 48tu4 39i63 39i63 um382 um238 r39ui r39ui	4fu89 4fu89 909h3 906h3 29dj2 29dj2 0emj3 0emj3	4t9i4 4t9i4 347h4 347h4 0k783 ok783 384h6 384h6
49tu4 49tu4 256ek 256ek 906i5 609i5 8nt84 8nt84	f48uf f48uf 489u3 489u3 398u4 938u4 6ru3j 6ru3j	209ru 209ru 9f3j7 9f3j7 j8grh j8grh fjr9f fjrf9	48t4j 48t4j f4j9a f4j9a 9k3h5 9k3h5 40kf8 40fk8
iu4yu iu4yu f48hd t48hd 902me 902me 908uy 908uy	4t8u4 4t8u4 90iy6 90iy6 6j87h 6j87h g7hi8 g7h8i	u8er3 u8er3 as8u1 as8u1 k945j k945j 049itr 049tir	4t8u4 4t8u4 90i73 90l73 49tui 49tui 9i5kg 9i5kg

Sheet 5

489ur4	489ru4	h9d39k	h9d39k	3er3uo	3eu3ro	t4j943	t4t943
73yre3	73yre3	mk9hd2	mk9dh2	dk392a	dk392a	39ri3h	39ri3h
09i5t5	09i5t5	ns2m1k	ns2m1k	9ih58f	9ih58f	d29jd0	d29jd0
4r9i32	4r9i32	je29h3	je29h3	rjk90r	rjk90r	9ui7yf	9ui7yf
9056k5	9056k5	58tu5j	58tu5j	45rf7y	54rf7y	4tioj4	4tioj4
384jr4	384jr4	t5j89t	f5j89t	98u76p	98u76p	26we20	26we20
37ye35	73ye35	9ik98u	9ik98u	87y45e	87y45e	r38u35	r83u35
94i54h	94i54h	j89jto	j89jto	h785r5	h785r5	d38ua3	d38ua3
5t8u53	5t8u53	4t94ia	4t94ia	4t84ua	4t84ua	tg489u	gt489u
e392sm	e392sm	38uf34	38uf34	398urk	398urk	h4978g	h4978g
0i48u4	0i48u4	90i3ka	9oi3ka	90i7yd	90l7yd	98yu4d	98yu4d
8u5n46	8v5n46	389uar	389uar	8uas2a	8uas2a	387ry3	387ry3
t58uf4	t58uf4	4t49ia	4t49ia	98u73h	98u37h	4t894u	4t894u
u90ir3	u90ir3	983yr3	938yr3	y767h3	y767h3	gf378y	gf378y
36tr3t	36fr3t	430ui4	430ui4	ui897n	ui897n	598ug5	598gu5
590i54	590i54	89u394	89u394	e3j82a	e3j82a	u578y5	u578y5
589ugt5	589ugt5	67h8g4	67h8g4	ei3984	ei3984	4t49if	4t49if
t498ut	t498ut	98u3j3	98u3j3	it949u	it499u	lly585	lly585
98uij4	98uij4	09i3j2	09l3j2	t84u8a	t84u8a	489irl	49i8rl
98u3e3	98v3e3	08u2e3	08u2e3	r389uf	r389uf	jr47lo	jr47lo
4t9u4k	4t9u4k	4t490if	4t490if	hg834j	hg834j	op5tiu	op5tiu
9fi34a	9fi34a	102ok3	102ok3	f4j9al	f4j9al	ti59um	ti59um
j9s2lk	j9s2lk	1946mj	1964mj	jd29aj	dj29aj	r4u8ny	r4u8ny
bnb832	bbn832	6k954r	6k954r	j93jad	j93jad	y9imy5	y6imy5
329jkf	329jkf	537974	537974	vxcmbf	vxcmbf	249uir	49uir
90if3j	9oif3j	453972	453792	teyuiq	teyuiq	da8d3k	da8d3k
907533	907533	529756	529756	pkldwh	pkldwh	9i3rnj	9i3nrj
etueom	etueom	537982	537982	opurjt	opvrjt	8j4nj5	8j4nj5

Sheet 6

7y9i 7y9i 7ty76 7ty76 64er 64re k90i k90i	r37y r37y fj38 fj38 gn48 gn48 hri3 hir3	538u 538u e38f e38f 64j6 64j6 c7bv c7vb	58m3 58m3 58c8 58c8 37yd 73yd d76t d76t
38uj 38uj nso9 sno9 bb49 bb49 p93u p93u	53uf 53uf tj49 tj49 as87 as87 ite4 Ite4	5378 5738 po38 po38 ju85 ju85 f74j f74j	4t49 4t49 fr3j fr3j d3h7 d3h7 89j4 98j4
r38u r38u 4r8u 4r8u c4m9 cm49 lt49 lt49	fe38 fe38 a389 a389 d38f d38f p39p p30p		

TEST 9

(Numerical Comparison)

(You will be given **150 questions** which should be completed using the time limit of **5 minutes**).

*Look at the four pairs of numerical digits. Circle or highlight the combination pair that **does not** match.*

Sheet 1

7956	7956	1494	1494	7964	9764	4956	4956
1697	1967	2987	2987	2985	2985	7895	7895
0948	0948	0575	0575	7956	7956	0958	0958
1897	1897	7974	7947	0987	0987	7439	7493
4852	4852	4478	4478	5578	5558	4475	7475
9635	9635	9369	9369	6991	6991	2265	2265
0087	8007	9885	9895	3578	3578	9018	9018
9954	9954	0058	0058	6998	6998	5837	5837
3375	3357	6652	6652	0894	0894	0950	9005
6695	6695	0573	5073	3984	3984	6952	6952
1058	1058	3985	3985	2584	5284	8945	8945
6789	6789	5568	5568	3999	3999	8509	8509
5904	5904	9765	9765	5944	5945	0914	0914
2984	9284	3941	9341	9568	9568	9716	9716
0595	0595	2993	2993	0948	0948	2980	2890
7906	7906	0958	0958	2947	2947	0589	0589
0954	0954	0594	0594	2984	2948	0593	0593
2595	2595	3987	3987	2929	2929	3958	3958
8974	8974	3982	3982	0847	0847	3914	3194
3982	3928	2958	9258	2966	2966	5984	5984
0395	0935	1497	1479	1974	1974	1904	1904
9454	9454	9846	9846	9507	9507	5095	5095
8709	8709	3944	3944	6675	6775	0634	0634
3047	3047	0985	0985	2901	2901	9877	8977
0084	0084	4897	8497	0595	0595	4235	4235
5971	5971	5907	5907	9635	9653	0985	0985
3895	3985	4795	4795	3356	3356	5774	5574
7915	7915	0974	0974	4108	4108	3699	3699

Look at the four pairs of numerical digits. Circle or highlight the combination pair that **does not** match.

Sheet 2

2595 2595	4797 4797	0593 0593	0294 0249
2947 2497	0924 9024	3947 3947	6597 6597
5923 5923	2953 2953	2956 2956	5696 5696
0894 0894	2987 2987	2947 2597	6958 6958

2946 2946	1905 1905	0259 0259	5094 5094
2394 2394	5987 5978	3954 3954	3295 3295
9875 9875	1996 1996	2978 2678	9785 9785
2935 9235	1993 1993	4974 4974	4591 4561

4189 4189	2098 2098	2094 2094	0259 2059
5987 5987	4597 4597	6987 6978	2944 2944
3291 2391	5936 5936	5698 5698	3987 3987
2934 2934	2694 2964	9085 9085	2390 2390

0295 0295	4086 4086	0954 0954	0589 0889
0098 0098	5940 5940	9594 9594	2954 2954
0798 7098	2395 2935	8977 8971	3987 3987
3698 3698	1095 1095	2596 2596	2391 2391

0259 0259	0594 0594	5094 5094	0956 0956
3985 3958	9564 9564	2394 2394	9054 9504
2597 2597	7958 7958	3987 3987	5984 5984
9804 9804	2987 9287	6030 6003	1904 1904

0594 0594	0594 0594	0496 0496	9504 6504
2950 2950	5587 5587	2987 2987	5954 5954
2597 2597	9957 9997	2956 2956	0905 0905
0955 9055	9939 9939	2978 2987	0957 0957

0956 0956	9054 9054	0595 0595	0595 0595
3965 3965	5987 5987	5988 5998	3985 3385
6958 6658	5953 5953	5986 5986	5978 5978
0295 0295	3958 5958	5945 5945	9698 9698

*Look at the four pairs of numerical digits. Circle or highlight the combination pair that **does not** match.*

Sheet 3

69547 69547	74585 74585	09548 09548	02951 02957
96325 96325	23658 23658	29047 29047	40847 40847
49525 49555	12549 12549	05953 05953	29857 29857
59878 59878	36589 39589	23984 23684	29846 29846

50951 50951	05954 05954	04805 04805	60595 60595
11153 17153	98987 68987	36985 36985	69989 69989
29822 29822	69535 69535	97452 91452	29643 26643
29234 29234	26878 26878	28901 28901	39515 39515

25905 52905	50954 50954	50995 50995	59546 59546
23954 23954	29847 29847	39656 39656	20957 20957
39624 39624	36694 36994	06910 90610	95086 90586
23698 23698	23945 23945	40958 40958	95807 95807

63095 63095	85098 85098	50624 50624	85406 85486
90584 90584	84561 84561	59065 59065	90586 90586
09547 09547	08214 08124	57098 57908	96541 96541
90584 09584	26255 26255	09556 09556	07567 07567

26047 62047	50695 50695	40564 40564	50845 50845
60508 60508	20954 20954	85408 85480	69067 69067
50631 50631	25956 26956	98078 98078	60484 60484
35068 35068	26987 26987	08996 08996	25605 25065

08554 08554	06546 06546	05984 05984	98054 98054
90588 90588	03987 03987	89048 80948	90545 90545
50678 56078	07900 09700	98494 98494	80056 08056
90544 90544	05605 05605	89686 89686	05651 05651

60314 60314	89404 89404	51404 51404	98404 98404
05416 05416	90667 90667	89598 89958	89509 89509
04544 04445	90596 90596	46908 46908	90784 90784
56654 56654	56897 56867	89407 89407	90636 90936

Look at the four pairs of numerical digits. Circle or highlight the combination pair that *does not* match.

Sheet 4

48945	48945	79465	79465	10498	01498	90223	90223
09854	09584	26887	26887	09874	09874	32246	32264
84709	84709	59505	59550	89584	89584	76948	76948
89781	89781	56512	56512	88950	88950	61236	61236

05465	05465	09464	09464	15647	15647	09984	09984
59879	59879	08978	08978	70956	70596	89098	89098
95042	95042	09858	09858	60589	60589	60352	60352
26205	26250	65048	65408	60470	60470	32223	32323

84989	84899	26556	26656	89463	89463	88596	88596
96583	96583	10069	10069	61256	67256	66587	66587
32653	32653	33208	33208	11520	11520	22513	52513
23878	23878	00689	00689	36625	36625	62320	62320

54098	54098	09569	09569	90594	90594	77469	77469
99686	99686	79561	79561	08059	08059	09594	09594
55858	55058	23952	23952	90544	90554	09596	09591
66521	66521	39589	39586	97865	97865	69889	69889

99687	96687	98056	98056	45904	45904	28841	28847
78974	78974	29057	29057	08459	08429	45848	45848
14564	14564	79532	79522	98785	98785	89049	89049
21894	21894	20958	20958	40889	40889	89745	89745

08484	08484	98584	98584	59065	59065	09459	09459
59097	59097	95657	95657	95409	95409	89748	89784
96456	96456	89535	89553	47485	47485	48148	48148
23234	32234	32654	32654	89484	99484	28977	28977

40984	40894	49088	49088	58094	58094	05945	05495
12898	12898	09589	09589	89477	89447	84708	84708
95957	95957	97095	97095	89096	89096	04965	04965
59589	59589	70589	10589	90562	90562	65468	65468

*Look at the four pairs of numerical digits. Circle or highlight the combination pair that **does not** match.*

Sheet 5

898489 898489	894086 894086	019840 019840	554787 554787
298945 299945	289787 289787	907464 907464	905458 905458
298454 298454	189465 819465	026923 026923	930487 930487
898745 898745	025615 025615	746286 746268	746489 146489

062594 062594	448796 448796	558965 558956	336098 336098
665897 665897	559863 559836	265497 265497	748501 748510
663254 663254	233658 233658	467985 467985	305698 305698
258898 259898	330559 330559	264258 264258	504136 504136

749865 749865	559865 558965	026035 026035	665478 665478
663259 663259	226589 226589	014897 014897	962015 926015
965832 695832	630552 630552	096354 096354	058469 058469
202001 202001	320598 320598	009850 009805	632985 632985

095362 095362	054815 084815	564189 564189	960228 960228
062548 062548	864556 864556	874987 874987	126213 126213
890847 860847	587484 587484	158856 518856	330698 336098
795623 795623	648654 648654	964784 964784	447856 447856

885698 885698	479566 479566	794613 974613	465236 465236
663352 663352	265977 265977	285963 285963	295695 295695
110231 110231	956632 956932	558963 558963	598978 598987
233312 238312	265231 265231	132597 132597	295210 295210

645684 645684	505862 805862	566985 569985	632095 632095
895983 895983	698563 698563	223652 223652	954876 954876
395988 395988	369561 369561	362015 362015	698563 698563
595623 559623	794623 794623	901582 901582	010530 070530

659589 659589	794613 794613	095887 095887	665045 665045
653215 653215	265896 265899	700589 700589	365952 365952
477856 471856	748513 748513	506057 506057	894751 894755
698554 698554	632569 632569	006086 606086	561315 561315

Look at the four pairs of numerical digits. Circle or highlight the combination pair that **does not** match.

Sheet 6

64685	46685	60958	60958	33041	33041	60474	60474
65461	65461	22054	22054	70523	70523	30659	30659
86486	86486	63025	63025	90852	90582	85896	85896
84962	84962	33021	32021	88320	88320	55671	56671

90874	90874	70956	70596	33065	33065	94064	94064
60365	60365	98056	98056	95957	95957	89798	89798
98988	98888	89455	89455	98562	98562	95632	59632
30044	30044	58451	58451	95623	95632	45215	45215

78946	78946	74956	74956
62302	62302	62647	62647
11326	31326	94160	64160
13035	13035	06959	06959

ANSWERS TO *TEST 9*

Sheet 1

7956	7956	1494	1494	7964	9764	4956	4956
1697	1967	2987	2987	2985	2985	7895	7895
0948	0948	0575	0575	7956	7956	0958	0958
1897	1897	7974	7947	0987	0987	7439	7493

4852	4852	4478	4478	5578	5558	4475	7475
9635	9635	9369	9369	6991	6991	2265	2265
0087	8007	9885	9895	3578	3578	9018	9018
9954	9954	0058	0058	6998	6998	5837	5837

3375	3357	6652	6652	0894	0894	0950	9005
6695	6695	0573	5073	3984	3984	6952	6952
1058	1058	3985	3985	2584	5284	8945	8945
6789	6789	5568	5568	3999	3999	8509	8509

5904	5904	9765	9765	5944	5945	0914	0914
2984	9284	3941	9341	9568	9568	9716	9716
0595	0595	2993	2993	0948	0948	2980	2890
7906	7906	0958	0958	2947	2947	0589	0589

0954	0954	0594	0594	2984	2948	0593	0593
2595	2595	3987	3987	2929	2929	3958	3958
8974	8974	3982	3982	0847	0847	3914	3194
3982	3928	2958	9258	2966	2966	5984	5984

0395	0935	1497	1479	1974	1974	1904	1904
9454	9454	9846	9846	9507	9507	5095	5095
8709	8709	3944	3944	6675	6775	0634	0634
3047	3047	0985	0985	2901	2901	9877	8977

0084	0084	4897	8497	0595	0595	4235	4235
5971	5971	5907	5907	9635	9653	0985	0985
3895	3985	4795	4795	3356	3356	5774	5574
7915	7915	0974	0974	4108	4108	3699	3699

Sheet 2

2595	2595	4797	4797	0593	0593	0294	0249
2947	2497	0924	9024	3947	3947	6597	6597
5923	5923	2953	2953	2956	2956	5696	5696
0894	0894	2987	2987	2947	2597	6958	6958

2946	2946	1905	1905	0259	0259	5094	5094
2394	2394	5987	5978	3954	3954	3295	3295
9875	9875	1996	1996	2978	2678	9785	9785
2935	9235	1993	1993	4974	4974	4591	4561

4189	4189	2098	2098	2094	2094	0259	2059
5987	5987	4597	4597	6987	6978	2944	2944
3291	2391	5936	5936	5698	5698	3987	3987
2934	2934	2694	2964	9085	9085	2390	2390

0295	0295	4086	4086	0954	0954	0589	0889
0098	0098	5940	5940	9594	9594	2954	2954
0798	7098	2395	2935	8977	8971	3987	3987
3698	3698	1095	1095	2596	2596	2391	2391

0259	0259	0594	0594	5094	5094	0956	0956
3985	3958	9564	9564	2394	2394	9054	9504
2597	2597	7958	7958	3987	3987	5984	5984
9804	9804	2987	9287	6030	6003	1904	1904

0594	0594	0594	0594	0496	0496	9504	6504
2950	2950	5587	5587	2987	2987	5954	5954
2597	2597	9957	9997	2956	2956	0905	0905
0955	9055	9939	9939	2978	2987	0957	0957

0956	0956	9054	9054	0595	0595	0595	0595
3965	3965	5987	5987	5988	5998	3985	3385
6958	6658	5953	5953	5986	5986	5978	5978
0295	0295	3958	5958	5945	5945	9698	9698

Sheet 3

69547 69547	74585 74585	09548 09548	02951 02957
96325 96325	23658 23658	29047 29047	40847 40847
49525 49555	12549 12549	05953 05953	29857 29857
59878 59878	36589 39589	23984 23684	29846 29846
50951 50951	05954 05954	04805 04805	60595 60595
11153 17153	98987 68987	36985 36985	69989 69989
29822 29822	69535 69535	97452 91452	29643 26643
29234 29234	26878 26878	28901 28901	39515 39515
25905 52905	50954 50954	50995 50995	59546 59546
23954 23954	29847 29847	39656 39656	20957 20957
39624 39624	36694 36994	06910 90610	95086 90586
23698 23698	23945 23945	40958 40958	95807 95807
63095 63095	85098 85098	50624 50624	85406 85486
90584 90584	84561 84561	59065 59065	90586 90586
09547 09547	08214 08124	57098 57908	96541 96541
90584 09584	26255 26255	09556 09556	07567 07567
26047 62047	50695 50695	40564 40564	50845 50845
60508 60508	20954 20954	85408 85480	69067 69067
50631 50631	25956 26956	98078 98078	60484 60484
35068 35068	26987 26987	08996 08996	25605 25065
08554 08554	06546 06546	05984 05984	98054 98054
90588 90588	03987 03987	89048 80948	90545 90545
50678 56078	07900 09700	98494 98494	80056 08056
90544 90544	05605 05605	89686 89686	05651 05651
60314 60314	89404 89404	51404 51404	98404 98404
05416 05416	90667 90667	89598 89958	89509 89509
04544 04445	90596 90596	46908 46908	90784 90784
56654 56654	56897 56867	89407 89407	90636 90936

Sheet 4

48945 48945	79465 79465	10498 01498	90223 90223
09854 09584	26887 26887	09874 09874	32246 32264
84709 84709	59505 59550	89584 89584	76948 76948
89781 89781	56512 56512	88950 88950	61236 61236
05465 05465	09464 09464	15647 15647	09984 09984
59879 59879	08978 08978	70956 70596	89098 89098
95042 95042	09858 09858	60589 60589	60352 60352
26205 26250	65048 65408	60470 60470	32223 32323
84989 84899	26556 26656	89463 89463	88596 88596
96583 96583	10069 10069	61256 67256	66587 66587
32653 32653	33208 33208	11520 11520	22513 52513
23878 23878	00689 00689	36625 36625	62320 62320
54098 54098	09569 09569	90594 90594	77469 77469
99686 99686	79561 79561	08059 08059	09594 09594
55858 55058	23952 23952	90544 90554	09596 09591
66521 66521	39589 39586	97865 97865	69889 69889
99687 96687	98056 98056	45904 45904	28841 28847
78974 78974	29057 29057	08459 08429	45848 45848
14564 14564	79532 79522	98785 98785	89049 89049
21894 21894	20958 20958	40889 40889	89745 89745
08484 08484	98584 98584	59065 59065	09459 09459
59097 59097	95657 95657	95409 95409	89748 89784
96456 96456	89535 89553	47485 47485	48148 48148
23234 32234	32654 32654	89484 99484	28977 28977
40984 40894	49088 49088	58094 58094	05945 05495
12898 12898	09589 09589	89477 89447	84708 84708
95957 95957	97095 97095	89096 89096	04965 04965
59589 59589	70589 10589	90562 90562	65468 65468

Sheet 5

898489 898489	894086 894086	019840 019840	554787 554787
298945 299945	289787 289787	907464 907464	905458 905458
298454 298454	189465 819465	026923 026923	930487 930487
898745 898745	025615 025615	746286 746268	746489 146489
062594 062594	448796 448796	558965 558956	336098 336098
665897 665897	559863 559836	265497 265497	748501 748510
663254 663254	233658 233658	467985 467985	305698 305698
258898 259898	330559 330559	264258 264258	504136 504136
749865 749865	559865 558965	026035 026035	665478 665478
663259 663259	226589 226589	014897 014897	962015 926015
965832 695832	630552 630552	096354 096354	058469 058469
202001 202001	320598 320598	009850 009805	632985 632985
095362 095362	054815 084815	564189 564189	960228 960228
062548 062548	864556 864556	874987 874987	126213 126213
890847 860847	587484 587484	158856 518856	330698 336098
795623 795623	648654 648654	964784 964784	447856 447856
885698 885698	479566 479566	794613 974613	465236 465236
663352 663352	265977 265977	285963 285963	295695 295695
110231 110231	956632 956932	558963 558963	598978 598987
233312 238312	265231 265231	132597 132597	295210 295210
645684 645684	505862 805862	566985 569985	632095 632095
895983 895983	698563 698563	223652 223652	954876 954876
395988 395988	369561 369561	362015 362015	698563 698563
595623 559623	794623 794623	901582 901582	010530 070530
659589 659589	794613 794613	095887 095887	665045 665045
653215 653215	265896 265899	700589 700589	365952 365952
477856 471856	748513 748513	506057 506057	894751 894755
698554 698554	632569 632569	006086 606086	561315 561315

Sheet 6

64685 46685	60958 60958	33041 33041	60474 60474
65461 65461	22054 22054	70523 70523	30659 30659
86486 86486	63025 63025	90852 90582	85896 85896
84962 84962	33021 32021	88320 88320	55671 56671
90874 90874	70956 70596	33065 33065	94064 94064
60365 60365	98056 98056	95957 95957	89798 89798
98988 98888	89455 89455	98562 98562	95632 59632
30044 30044	58451 58451	95623 95632	45215 45215
78946 78946	74956 74956		
62302 62302	62647 62647		
11326 31326	94160 64160		
13035 13035	06959 06959		

TEST 10

(Alpha-Numerical Comparison)

(You will be given **150 questions** which should be completed using the time limit of **5 minutes**).

Look at the four pairs of alpha-numerical digits. Circle or highlight the combination pair that **does not** match.

Sheet 1

44u0	44n0	k05g	k05g	0r49	0r49	3ei9	3ei9
59yj	59yj	f9ui	f9ui	3e8u	3e8u	04or	04or
g5i9	g5i9	ao0w	a0ow	239i	329i	49ut	49ut
f490	f490	w20o	w20o	d20n	d20n	plt1	pit1
7hg4	7hg4	2w7y	2w7y	lc93	lc93	o9r4	o9r4
r3io	r3oi	3r8u	3r8u	uie9	eiu9	48ur	48ur
cmov	cmov	c3m9	c3n9	ry83	ry83	mv49	mu49
tri9	tri9	dh38	dh38	x73n	x73n	d38h	d38h
ir3e	lr3e	w1t6	w1t6	f48u	f48u	x6v8	x6v8
r3u8	r3u8	qp19	qp19	e387	e387	n8v7	n8v7
k837	k837	19wi	91wi	0c38	0c83	d78g	d78g
32r3	32r3	cm37	cm37	38e7	38e7	g94p	p94q
f84u	f84u	y48u	y48u	3tr7	3tr7	49tr	49tr
9iy5	9iy5	t4y7	t4y7	409i	409i	r37y	r37y
w25r	w25r	0oe2	o0e2	vm38	vm83	gm9r	gm9r
bm39	bm36	mcp3	mcp3	ek49	ek49	r39u	r39v
x2m9	x2m9	f49i	f49i	4tru	4tru	a10o	a10o
d392	d392	cv4m	cu4m	f48y	t48y	c3k9	c3k9
l0d3	l0d3	d3j9	d3j9	c4m8	c4m8	x8b0	x8bo
39ie	39ei	38ud	38ud	pl58	pl58	mbjf	mbjf
4k9c	4k9c	cm9e	cm9e	b3nu	b3nu	c378	c378
39ie	39ie	zp3l	zq3l	x395	x395	5397	5739
0odf	o0df	w129	w129	g49i	g49l	smbf	smbf
aleo	aleo	akdj	akdj	z3k0	z3k0	efue	efue
fu8e	fu8e	4rt7	4rt7	mc39	mc39	cvb4	cvb4
39r5	39r5	3n6i	3n6i	j494	j494	dgji	dgji
0c83	0c83	f8e7	f8a7	ad8y	da8y	g4u9	g4b9
78m6	87m6	38oa	38oa	9ujf	9ujf	k38a	k38a

*Look at the four pairs of alpha-numerical digits. Circle or highlight the combination pair that **does not** match.*

Sheet 2

4ti0	4ti0	f348	f348	v4m9	v4m9	ad89	ad89
3e39	3e39	dwor	dwor	asfi	asfi	cmdi	cndi
d39a	d39a	alcj	aicj	xa8a	xa8a	sal3	sal3
bv5u	bu5u	gdfs	gdfs	caj8	cal8	xej9	xej9
gt4u	gt4u	u48u	u48u	4mf8	4mf8	3d9v	3d9v
ajsi	ajsi	3572	3572	xc7a	xc7a	0n8s	0n8s
hsj8	hsj8	539f	593f	a6d9	a6d6	df69	dt69
fa86	fe86	4h6o	4h6o	v9n8	v9n8	g7d3	g7d3
x5c7	x5c7	4tf8	4tf8	4e70	4e70	r37y	r37y
m0b8	m0b8	e8a7	e8a7	0y94	0y94	9sa4	9sa4
a46d	a46b	a870	a870	4732	4732	ei92	el92
hg89	hg89	n90d	n90b	r839	r893	v0o8	v0o8
47ft	47ft	q4e6	q4e6	w62t	w62t	er35	er35
h58u	h58u	w8rm	w8rn	59it	59it	y56i	y56i
cv4j	cv4l	mxz8	mxz8	f49s	f49s	iyto	iyto
ak0l	ak0l	de89	de89	d323	d332	lyjg	lygj
r37y	r37y	q49i	q49i	q7y3	q7y3	ncvn	ncvn
yi59	yi95	asdu	asdv	ek39	ek39	dkjg	dkjg
dma9	dma9	5989	5989	sa83	sa38	eori	eorl
cm42	cm42	4309	4309	fm94	fm94	adlk	adlk
389r	389r	e48a	e48a	w7ya	w7ya	cmcj	cmcj
xdaj	xdaj	dkfa	dkfa	s9ui	s9iu	erjd	erjd
4098	4098	lkpo	lkop	ak0s	ak0s	asdk	asdk
35rj	53rj	pod8	pod8	dk39	dk39	ewlo	welo
oe83	oe83	k348	k348	4j9a	4j9a	04jd	o4jd
34ra	34ra	ada9	ada9	9uia	9uia	7d9g	7d9g
ia93	la93	qejo	pejo	as93	sa93	3a5f	3a5f
ska9	ska9	dakl	dakl	dak0	dak0	g3ma	g3ma

*Look at the four pairs of alpha-numerical digits. Circle or highlight the combination pair that **does not** match.*

Sheet 3

834ur	834ur	238dk	238dk	alksf	alksf	39d77	39d77
3daik	3daik	ds73n	ds73n	r3887	r3887	7as02	7as02
fsjk3	fslk3	cl3m7	cl3m7	oieue	oieue	92ma8	92na8
da47f	da47f	a9s7w	a9s7u	vcbnm	vabnm	a9dm7	a9dm7
w4e6t	we46t	j84ld	j84ld	266ta	266ta	mxcna	mxcna
mlp96	mlp96	k9d3a	k9d3a	cd3k9	cd3k9	ksjdr	ksjdr
uip74	uip74	mc83n	mc83a	mcvnd	mcved	kj38h	jk38h
4m3gp	4m3gp	c8v39	c8v39	r39as	r39as	d83an	d83an
opela	opela	mxcvn	mxcun	38eus	38eus	c3m8d	c3m8d
as892	as892	gdik4	gdik4	d39tr	d39tr	er39k	er93k
29348	29438	h7d30	h7d30	t4fue	t4feu	f3j8d	f3j8d
awklr	awklr	d38jf	d38jf	e38sn	e38sn	vm48a	vm48a
3f8ur	3f8ur	cv94m	vc94m	r387d	r387d	43m5k	43m5k
r3u8s	r3u8s	43j8a	43j8a	384u3	348u3	6m4b3	6m4b3
f3uda	f3uda	83j8l	83j8l	2bh5k	2bh5k	3v45k	v345k
t38ur	t38ru	8ut34	8ut34	t5j3g	t5j3g	7n5h4	7n5h4
3m69d	3m66d	4rjas	4rjas	8tk5u	8tk5u	347m3	347m3
a37n5	a37n5	d3j8s	d3j8s	3h5k6	3h5k6	7no47	7no47
5bn38	5bn38	4r8rk	r48rk	6m4n4	6m4n4	6nh3g	6hn3g
0l28d	0l28d	u3m7k	u3m7k	3h21b	3h21d	43j2h	43j2h
4r8ud	4r8ud	2376n	2376n	h37yd	h37yd	w26tr	w26tr
d3asn	d3asn	3n5b6	3b5n6	f48oi	f48oi	t458u	t458u
39sa3	39sa3	7mk56	7mk56	opo38	poo38	b7v4i	b7v4i
ew2ie	we2ie	4h3j6	4h3j6	dj3n5	dj3n5	l38ja	i38ja
4fr7y	4fr7y	fn83d	fn83d	qt16o	qt16o	2w8uf	2w8uf
fj3as	fj3as	vmr3a	vmr3a	e39ir	e39ri	m4f8d	m4f8d
d2k9a	dk29a	sfhjk	shfjk	mvc9r	mvc9r	po38f	po3f8
oke28	oke28	eiotu	eiotu	fdkj4	fdkj4	34k6h	34k6h

*Look at the four pairs of alpha-numerical digits. Circle or highlight the combination pair that **does not** match.*

Sheet 4

r47yd	r47yd	26wt9	26wt9	3h58g	3h58g	a34s6	a34s6
e39if	e39if	i4n3b	i4n3b	5k7pl	k57pl	d6g9b	d6g9b
fdm30	fmd30	u3ja8	u3ja8	8k5b3	8k5b3	c6v8n	c6v8n
d3ma7	d3ma7	y23na	y23an	23bvn	23bvn	v76s4	u76s4

r93i7	r93i7	w2h4k	w2h4k	p38yu	p38yu	l8u4k	l8u4k
vcm4b	vcm4b	65n4h	65n4h	39857	35987	dj3d7	dj3d7
fj84d	fl84d	3g4hs	3g4hs	wdjek	wdjek	jgmo2	gjmo2
plw93	plw93	c0b9f	cbo9f	3nahs	3nahs	ekld3	ekld3

fj349	fj349	3ryk2	3ryk2	6ne8p	6ne8p	cmvnj	cmvnj
6lp7m	6pl7m	1apw1	1apw1	0oo0o	0oo0o	letud	letud
5m5b3	5m5b3	0s9f7	0sf97	tk3hj	tk3hj	eorud	eroud
3b5n6	3b5n6	0o9op	0o9op	35987	35897	eoitu	eoitu

d378y	d378y	w4e56	w4e56	q1tr7	q1tr7	lp49f	lp49f
jxd89	jxd89	t6y7u	t6y7u	0or38	0or38	r3u8e	r3u8e
adhjh	dahjh	i987y	i987u	c38fu	c38fu	cvnb8	cvmb8
fn4ls	fn4ls	m3bn6	m3bn6	s49ow	s49wo	rn2ma	rn2ma

3e8ud	3e8ud	q10or	q10or	pl3o9	pl3o9	xm39g	xm39g
17840	17840	c8v0n	c8v0n	f8ure	f8ure	gok38	gok38
53072	53072	f8hq1	f8h1q	398dk	389dk	3md89	3md98
429k4	492k4	plq1a	plq1a	dmw38	dmw38	f39uf	f39uf

4tr8u	4tr8u	6t79i	6t79i	27wy9	27wy9	w7y9e	w7y9e
20skf	02skf	2ebc3	2ebc3	r3uvn	r3uvn	38un3	38un3
30kv8	30kv8	mr3k9	rm3k9	f3i9a	f3ia9	r3ki9	r3k9i
v90k3	v90k3	eplf8	eplf8	pl38d	pl38d	cb37g	cb37g

38uro	38uro	q10oe	q10oe	3re78	3re78	3e7ya	3e7ya
39c3n	39c3n	r34i9	r349i	v239r	v923r	w91ma	w91ma
i3do2	i3od2	vnb94	vnb94	9ie24	9ie24	c893m	c893n
pl2sk	pl2sk	d38dg	d38dg	epl39	epl39	e0ory	e0ory

*Look at the four pairs of alpha-numerical digits. Circle or highlight the combination pair that **does not** match.*

Sheet 5

v4jf	v4jf	38ru	38ru	cm94	cm94	bcvf	bcvf
f349	f349	40kv	40kv	vg4j9	vg4j9	kdgj	kdjg
w38e	w38a	37yt	37ut	39ru	39ru	foet	foet
8u3e	8u3e	4n8c	4n8c	d30i	d3oi	gkde	gkde
x3m9	x3m9	w2u8	w2u8	37ry	37ry	3f8u	3f8v
h4j9	h4j9	t4ui	t4ui	f34m	f34m	9jgy	9jgy
g48u	g48v	vn48	vn48	mc39	mc93	t48y	t48y
r39i	r39i	hg48	hg84	dk03	dk03	fn38	fn38
cn38	cn38	48ru	48ru	f48u	f48u	3694	3694
x3m9	x3m6	vm48	vm48	vm48	mv48	iojt	iojt
fk39	fk39	38ua	83ua	d3j8	d3j8	t9e0	t90e
39ru	39ru	3957	3957	wori	wori	e9ir	e9ir
4u8f	u48f	4r89	4r89	a129	a129	27wy	27wy
f38u	f38u	39m3	39m3	q198	q198	94ir	94ir
53fj	53fj	7kh5	7hk5	3e9i	3ei9	r3m9	r3n9
wope	wope	9gj1	9gj1	r3uf	r3uf	38ur	38ur
3r8u	3r8u	q1u8	q1u8	39ei	39ei	48uf	48uf
49pi	49pi	e3u8	e3u8	cm39	cm39	3957	3057
oi87	oi78	mc48	cm48	jf38	jf38	4290	4290
kj76	kj76	r3h8	r3h8	dslr	dlsr	1m1o	1m1o
p4jl	p4jl	vbcm	vbcm	xm39	xm39	4t8u	4t8u
t3k9	t3k9	lakd	lakd	3mc9	3mc9	fv38	fv83
e2i9	e29i	pxme	pxme	3uep	8uep	cn37	cn37
5i94	5i94	meuc	muec	3l9d	3l9d	aslk	aslk
h8g4	h8g4	q1o0	q1o0	2e9v	2e9v	cm39	cm39
k9lj	k9ij	19qi	79qi	49if	49if	vf4t	vf4t
pipo	pipo	wi1r	wi1r	r9ia	r9ai	t498	t498
oiok	oiok	81qw	81qw	d9ie	d9ie	38ru	83ru

*Look at the four pairs of alpha-numerical digits. Circle or highlight the combination pair that **does not** match.*

Sheet 6

38rdi0 38rdi0	110l1s 110l1s	o0olam o0olam	2w9jda 2w9jda
282ms2 228ms2	sal19a sal19a	a9c8b7 a9c8b7	439djf 439djf
2d0o3d 2d0o3d	10alac 10aalc	v7as69 v7sa69	9vub87 9vvb87
0ck8fj 0ck8fj	cm180a cm180a	iulo91 iulo91	28dasj 28dasj

3e8yud 3e8yud	cm39fu cm39fu	x3m9zl x3m9zl	vm39gh vm39gh
asm878 asm878	weporu weporu	asl29a asl29a	alsk38 alsk38
d09i2a do9i2a	alskhf alskfh	polo87 polo78	39dk37 93dk37
s2isl1 s2isl1	cmvnjf cmvnjf	29dk38 29dk38	1m4n6b 1m4n6b

48ruam 48ruam	2e9idm 2e9dim
3d8ual 3d8ual	gm39fh gm39fh
29ap1l 29ap1l	d238ua d238ua
1msjf8 1msfj8	239idl 239idl

ANSWERS TO *TEST 10*

Sheet 1

44u0 44n0	k05g k05g	0r49 0r49	3ei9 3ei9
59yj 59yj	f9ui f9ui	3e8u 3e8u	04or 04or
g5i9 g5i9	ao0w a0ow	239i 329i	49ut 49ut
f490 f490	w20o w20o	d20n d20n	plt1 pit1
7hg4 7hg4	2w7y 2w7y	lc93 lc93	o9r4 o9r4
r3io r3oi	3r8u 3r8u	uie9 eiu9	48ur 48ur
cmov cmov	c3m9 c3n9	ry83 ry83	mv49 mu49
tri9 tri9	dh38 dh38	x73n x73n	d38h d38h
ir3e lr3e	w1t6 w1t6	f48u f48u	x6v8 x6v8
r3u8 r3u8	qp19 qp19	e387 e387	n8v7 n8v7
k837 k837	19wi 91wi	0c38 0c83	d78g d78g
32r3 32r3	cm37 cm37	38e7 38e7	g94p p94q
f84u f84u	y48u y48u	3tr7 3tr7	49tr 49tr
9iy5 9iy5	t4y7 t4y7	409i 409i	r37y r37y
w25r w25r	0oe2 o0e2	vm38 vm83	gm9r gm9r
bm39 bm36	mcp3 mcp3	ek49 ek49	r39u r39v
x2m9 x2m9	f49i f49i	4tru 4tru	a10o a10o
d392 d392	cv4m cu4m	f48y t48y	c3k9 c3k9
l0d3 l0d3	d3j9 d3j9	c4m8 c4m8	x8b0 x8bo
39ie 39ei	38ud 38ud	pl58 pl58	mbjf mbjf
4k9c 4k9c	cm9e cm9e	b3nu b3nu	c378 c378
39ie 39ie	zp3l zq3l	x395 x395	5397 5739
0odf o0df	w129 w129	g49i g49l	smbf smbf
aleo aleo	akdj akdj	z3k0 z3k0	efue efue
fu8e fu8e	4rt7 4rt7	mc39 mc39	cvb4 cvb4
39r5 39r5	3n6i 3n6i	j494 j494	dgji dgji
0c83 0c83	f8e7 f8a7	ad8y da8y	g4u9 g4b9
78m6 87m6	38oa 38oa	9ujf 9ujf	k38a k38a

Sheet 2

4ti0 4ti0	f348 f348	v4m9 v4m9	ad89 ad89
3e39 3e39	dwor dwor	asfi asfi	cmdi cndi
d39a d39a	alcj aicj	xa8a xa8a	sal3 sal3
bv5u bu5u	gdfs gdfs	caj8 cal8	xej9 xej9
gt4u gt4u	u48u u48u	4mf8 4mf8	3d9v 3d9v
ajsi ajsi	3572 3572	xc7a xc7a	0n8s 0n8s
hsj8 hsj8	539f 593f	a6d9 a6d6	df69 dt69
fa86 fe86	4h6o 4h6o	v9n8 v9n8	g7d3 g7d3
x5c7 x5c7	4tf8 4tf8	4e70 4e70	r37y r37y
m0b8 m0b8	e8a7 e8a7	0y94 0y94	9sa4 9sa4
a46d a46b	a870 a870	4732 4732	ei92 el92
hg89 hg89	n90d n90b	r839 r893	v0o8 v0o8
47ft 47ft	q4e6 q4e6	w62t w62t	er35 er35
h58u h58u	w8rm w8rn	59it 59it	y56i y56i
cv4j cv4l	mxz8 mxz8	f49s f49s	iyto iyto
ak0l ak0l	de89 de89	d323 d332	lyjg lygj
r37y r37y	q49i q49i	q7y3 q7y3	ncvn ncvn
yi59 yi95	asdu asdv	ek39 ek39	dkjg dkjg
dma9 dma9	5989 5989	sa83 sa38	eori eorl
cm42 cm42	4309 4309	fm94 fm94	adlk adlk
389r 389r	e48a e48a	w7ya w7ya	cmcj cmcj
xdaj xdaj	dkfa dkfa	s9ui s9iu	erjd erjd
4098 4098	lkpo lkop	ak0s ak0s	asdk asdk
35rj 53rj	pod8 pod8	dk39 dk39	ewlo welo
oe83 oe83	k348 k348	4j9a 4j9a	04jd o4jd
34ra 34ra	ada9 ada9	9uia 9uia	7d9g 7d9g
ia93 la93	qejo pejo	as93 sa93	3a5f 3a5f
ska9 ska9	dakl dakl	dak0 dak0	g3ma g3ma

Sheet 3

834ur 834ur	238dk 238dk	alksf alksf	39d77 39d77
3daik 3daik	ds73n ds73n	r3887 r3887	7as02 7as02
fsjk3 fslk3	cl3m7 cl3m7	oieue oieue	92ma8 92na8
da47f da47f	a9s7w a9s7u	vcbnm vabnm	a9dm7 a9dm7

w4e6t we46t	j84ld j84ld	266ta 266ta	mxcna mxcna
mlp96 mlp96	k9d3a k9d3a	cd3k9 cd3k9	ksjdr ksjdr
uip74 uip74	mc83n mc83a	mcvnd mcved	kj38h jk38h
4m3gp 4m3gp	c8v39 c8v39	r39as r39as	d83an d83an

opela opela	mxcvn mxcun	38eus 38eus	c3m8d c3m8d
as892 as892	gdik4 gdik4	d39tr d39tr	er39k er93k
29348 29438	h7d30 h7d30	t4fue t4feu	f3j8d f3j8d
awklr awklr	d38jf d38jf	e38sn e38sn	vm48a vm48a

3f8ur 3f8ur	cv94m vc94m	r387d r387d	43m5k 43m5k
r3u8s r3u8s	43j8a 43j8a	384u3 348u3	6m4b3 6m4b3
f3uda f3uda	83j8l 83j8l	2bh5k 2bh5k	3v45k v345k
t38ur t38ru	8ut34 8ut34	t5j3g t5j3g	7n5h4 7n5h4

3m69d 3m66d	4rjas 4rjas	8tk5u 8tk5u	347m3 347m3
a37n5 a37n5	d3j8s d3j8s	3h5k6 3h5k6	7no47 7no47
5bn38 5bn38	4r8rk r48rk	6m4n4 6m4n4	6nh3g 6hn3g
0l28d 0l28d	u3m7k u3m7k	3h21b 3h21d	43j2h 43j2h

4r8ud 4r8ud	2376n 2376n	h37yd h37yd	w26tr w26tr
d3asn d3asn	3n5b6 3b5n6	f48oi f48oi	t458u t458u
39sa3 39sa3	7mk56 7mk56	opo38 poo38	b7v4i b7v4i
ew2ie we2ie	4h3j6 4h3j6	dj3n5 dj3n5	l38ja i38ja

4fr7y 4fr7y	fn83d fn83d	qt16o qt16o	2w8uf 2w8uf
fj3as fj3as	vmr3a vmr3a	e39ir e39ri	m4f8d m4f8d
d2k9a dk29a	sfhjk shfjk	mvc9r mvc9r	po38f po3f8
oke28 oke28	eiotu eiotu	fdkj4 fdkj4	34k6h 34k6h

Sheet 4

r47yd r47yd e39if e39if fdm30 fmd30 d3ma7 d3ma7	26wt9 26wt9 i4n3b i4n3b u3ja8 u3ja8 y23na y23an	3h58g 3h58g 5k7pl k57pl 8k5b3 8k5b3 23bvn 23bvn	a34s6 a34s6 d6g9b d6g9b c6v8n c6v8n v76s4 u76s4
r93i7 r93i7 vcm4b vcm4b fj84d fl84d plw93 plw93	w2h4k w2h4k 65n4h 65n4h 3g4hs 3g4hs c0b9f cbo9f	p38yu p38yu 39857 35987 wdjek wdjek 3nahs 3nahs	l8u4k l8u4k dj3d7 dj3d7 jgmo2 gjmo2 ekld3 ekld3
fj349 fj349 6lp7m 6pl7m 5m5b3 5m5b3 3b5n6 3b5n6	3ryk2 3ryk2 1apw1 1apw1 0s9f7 0sf97 0o9op 0o9op	6ne8p 6ne8p 0oo0o 0oo0o tk3hj tk3hj 35987 35897	cmvnj cmvnj letud letud eorud eroud eoitu eoitu
d378y d378y jxd89 jxd89 adhjh dahjh fn4ls fn4ls	w4e56 w4e56 t6y7u t6y7u i987y i987u m3bn6 m3bn6	q1tr7 q1tr7 0or38 0or38 c38fu c38fu s49ow s49wo	lp49f lp49f r3u8e r3u8e cvnb8 cvmb8 rn2ma rn2ma
3e8ud 3e8ud 17840 17840 53072 53072 429k4 492k4	q10or q10or c8v0n c8v0n f8hq1 f8h1q plq1a plq1a	pl3o9 pl3o9 f8ure f8ure 398dk 389dk dmw38 dmw38	xm39g xm39g gok38 gok38 3md89 3md98 f39uf f39uf
4tr8u 4tr8u 20skf 02skf 30kv8 30kv8 v90k3 v90k3	6t79i 6t79i 2ebc3 2ebc3 mr3k9 rm3k9 eplf8 eplf8	27wy9 27wy9 r3uvn r3uvn f3i9a f3ia9 pl38d pl38d	w7y9e w7y9e 38un3 38un3 r3ki9 r3k9i cb37g cb37g
38uro 38uro 39c3n 39c3n i3do2 i3od2 pl2sk pl2sk	q10oe q10oe r34i9 r349i vnb94 vnb94 d38dg d38dg	3re78 3re78 v239r v923r 9ie24 9ie24 epl39 epl39	3e7ya 3e7ya w91ma w91ma c893m c893n e0ory e0ory

Sheet 5

v4jf	v4jf	38ru	38ru	cm94	cm94	bcvf	bcvf
f349	f349	40kv	40kv	vg4j9	vg4j9	kdgj	kdjg
w38e	w38a	37yt	37ut	39ru	39ru	foet	foet
8u3e	8u3e	4n8c	4n8c	d30i	d3oi	gkde	gkde
x3m9	x3m9	w2u8	w2u8	37ry	37ry	3f8u	3f8v
h4j9	h4j9	t4ui	t4ui	f34m	f34m	9jgy	9jgy
g48u	g48v	vn48	vn48	mc39	mc93	t48y	t48y
r39i	r39i	hg48	hg84	dk03	dk03	fn38	fn38
cn38	cn38	48ru	48ru	f48u	f48u	3694	3694
x3m9	x3m6	vm48	vm48	vm48	mv48	iojt	iojt
fk39	fk39	38ua	83ua	d3j8	d3j8	t9e0	t90e
39ru	39ru	3957	3957	wori	wori	e9ir	e9ir
4u8f	u48f	4r89	4r89	a129	a129	27wy	27wy
f38u	f38u	39m3	39m3	q198	q198	94ir	94ir
53fj	53fj	7kh5	7hk5	3e9i	3ei9	r3m9	r3n9
wope	wope	9gj1	9gj1	r3uf	r3uf	38ur	38ur
3r8u	3r8u	q1u8	q1u8	39ei	39ei	48uf	48uf
49pi	49pi	e3u8	e3u8	cm39	cm39	3957	3057
oi87	oi78	mc48	cm48	jf38	jf38	4290	4290
kj76	kj76	r3h8	r3h8	dslr	dlsr	1m1o	1m1o
p4jl	p4jl	vbcm	vbcm	xm39	xm39	4t8u	4t8u
t3k9	t3k9	lakd	lakd	3mc9	3mc9	fv38	fv83
e2i9	e29i	pxme	pxme	3uep	8uep	cn37	cn37
5i94	5i94	meuc	muec	3l9d	3l9d	aslk	aslk
h8g4	h8g4	q1o0	q1o0	2e9v	2e9v	cm39	cm39
k9lj	k9ij	19qi	79qi	49if	49if	vf4t	vf4t
pipo	pipo	wi1r	wi1r	r9ia	r9ai	t498	t498
oiok	oiok	81qw	81qw	d9ie	d9ie	38ru	83ru

Sheet 6

38rdi0 38rdi0 282ms2 228ms2 2d0o3d 2d0o3d 0ck8fj 0ck8fj	110l1s 110l1s sal19a sal19a 10alac 10aalc cm180a cm180a	o0olam o0olam a9c8b7 a9c8b7 v7as69 v7sa69 iulo91 iulo91	2w9jda 2w9jda 439djf 439djf 9vub87 9vvb87 28dasj 28dasj
3e8yud 3e8yud asm878 asm878 d09i2a do9i2a s2isl1 s2isl1	cm39fu cm39fu weporu weporu alskhf alskfh cmvnjf cmvnjf	x3m9zl x3m9zl asl29a asl29a polo87 polo78 29dk38 29dk38	vm39gh vm39gh alsk38 alsk38 39dk37 93dk37 1m4n6b 1m4n6b
48ruam 48ruam 3d8ual 3d8ual 29ap1l 29ap1l 1msjf8 1msfj8	2e9idm 2e9dim gm39fh gm39fh d238ua d238ua 239idl 239idl		

A FEW FINAL WORDS...

You have now reached the end of your Numerical Concentration Testing guide. Hopefully now, you should feel more comfortable and confident to tackle your assessment, and understand the expectations and requirements to successfully pass your Numerical Concentration Test.

For any psychometric test, there are a few things to remember which will help you perform at your best:

REMEMBER – THE THREE P'S!

1. **Prepare.** This may seem relatively obvious, but you will be surprised by how many people fail psychometric testing because they lacked the knowledge and understanding of what to expect. Be sure to practice these tests before having to sit the real test. Not only will you become familiar with the testing questions, it will also take off some of the pressure leading up to that all important test. Like anything, the more you practice, the more likely you are to succeed!

2. **Perseverance.** You are far more likely to succeed at something if you continuously set out to achieve it. Everybody comes across times where they are setback or find obstacles in the way of their goals. The important thing to remember when this happens, is to use those setbacks and obstacles as a way of progressing. It is what you do with your past experiences that helps to determine your success in the future. If you fail at something, consider 'why' you have failed. This will allow you to improve and enhance your performance for the next time.

3. **Performance.** Performance is a great word. Your performance will determine whether or not you are likely to succeed. Attributes that are often associated with performance are self-belief, motivation and commitment. Self-belief is important for anything you do in your life. It allows you to recognise your own abilities and skills, and believe that you can do well. Believing that you can do well is half the battle! Being fully motivated and committed is often difficult for some people, but we can assure you that, nothing is gained without hard work and determination. If you want to succeed, you will need to put in that extra time and hard work!

The majority of candidates who pass the selection process for their chosen career have a number of common attributes. These are as follows:

1. They believe in themselves.

The first factor is self-belief. Regardless of what anyone tells you, you can pass your tests and get the job that you really want. Just like any test, interview or selection process, you have to be prepared to work hard in order to be successful. Make sure you have the self-belief to pass the psychometric tests with high scores and fill your mind with positive thoughts.

2. They prepare fully.

The second factor is preparation. Those people who achieve in life prepare fully for every eventuality, and that is what you must do when you prepare for your Numerical Concentration Test. Work very hard and especially concentrate on your weak areas.

3. They are self-motivated.

How much do you want this job? Do you want it, or do you really want it? When you apply for any job you should want it more than anything in the world. Your levels of self-motivation will shine through on your application, whilst sitting the test and also, during your interview. For the weeks and months leading up to the selection process, be motivated as best you can and always keep your fitness levels up, as this will serve to increase your levels of motivation.

Work hard, stay focused and be what you want.

Remember, we have also provided you with some additional free online psychometric tests which will help to further improve your competence in this particular testing area. To gain access, simply go to:

www.PsychometricTestsOnline.co.uk

Good luck with your Numerical Concentration Test. We wish you the best of luck with all your future endeavours!

The how2become team

The How2become team

how2become

Get more books, manuals, online tests and training courses at:

www.How2Become.com